"This volume is chock-full of practical insights on how church leaders can free up more money for the real mission of the church—our impact *beyond* the church in helping people live better lives. The counterintuitive suggestions are just spot on."

—**Reggie McNeal**, author of *Get Off Your Donkey!*

"This book speaks my love language! The old ministry paradigm—'*find a need and fill it*'—produces overextended and unfocused churches, diluting local church impact. The new mantra for church health is '*less is more.*' The problem with many churches today isn't a shortage of ministries, staff, buildings, or finances—but an abundance of all these resources that are overprogrammed, underutilized, or poorly managed. *The More-with-Less Church* shows you how to fully maximize your church's resources to fulfill its mission and vision. Don't start another program, hire another staff member, lay another brick, or raise another dollar until you read this book!"

—**Jim Tomberlin**, founder and senior strategist, MultiSite Solutions; author of *125 Tips for Multisite Churches, Better Together,* and *Church Locality*

"As the new pastor of a church that was nearly seventy-five years old with a history of struggles, I was excited that the church was growing and good things were happening but overwhelmed by the many voices telling us what next steps to take. Among our leaders there was no clear sense of what we needed to do when it came to our facility, finances, ministries, and staffing. Some wanted to build, but the church was still saddled with debt. Partnering with Living Stones was the most providential moment for our church, as they gave us tremendously helpful insight in all of these areas as well as how to help our church become even healthier. Our two planning processes with them helped us to more than double our attendance over the next eight years without adding one square inch of space, to eliminate our ⟨ ⟩ y and staffing, and to set oursel⟨v⟩ tiveness in our ministries. *The More-with-Less Church* now makes available to a much wider audience the principles that have been so life-giving for Riverside. I thank the Lord for the ministry of Living Stones and how God used them to help us in an amazingly comprehensive way."

—**Tom Lundeen**, senior pastor, Riverside Church,
Big Lake, Minnesota

"The conventional church growth wisdom calls for bigger, bigger, bigger. Bigger staff, bigger budgets, bigger buildings. *The More-with-Less Church* is different. It flips the dominant paradigm on its head and shows it's actually possible to impact more people without breaking the budget or burning out your staff. The authors are not ivory tower theoreticians. They've served in the trenches of ministry and walked alongside hundreds of other church leaders. Their ideas are field-tested and practical. As you read this valuable book, you'll soon be seeing ways you can employ these principles to be more faithful and effective in your ministry."

—**Drew Dyck**, managing editor of *Leadership Journal*
and author of *Yawning at Tigers: You Can't
Tame God, So Stop Trying*

THE
MORE
—WITH—
LESS
CHURCH

Maximize Your Money, Space, Time,
and People to Multiply Ministry Impact

**EDDY HALL, RAY BOWMAN,
AND J. SKIPP MACHMER**

BakerBooks
a division of Baker Publishing Group
Grand Rapids, Michigan

© 2014 by Eddy Hall and Ray Bowman

Published by Baker Books
a division of Baker Publishing Group
P.O. Box 6287, Grand Rapids, MI 49516-6287
www.bakerbooks.com

Printed in the United States of America

Library of Congress Cataloging-in-Publication Data
Hall, Eddy.
    The more-with-less church : maximize your money, space, time, and people to multiply ministry impact / Eddy Hall, Ray Bowman, and J. Skipp Machmer.
        pages cm
    Includes bibliographical references.
    ISBN 978-0-8010-1553-3 (pbk.)
    1. Church management. 2. Church growth. I. Title.
BV652.H28 2014
254—dc23   2014012050

Unless otherwise indicated, Scripture quotations are from The Holy Bible, English Standard Version® (ESV®), copyright © 2001 by Crossway, a publishing ministry of Good News Publishers. Used by permission. All rights reserved. ESV Text Edition: 2007

Scripture quotations labeled CEV are from the Contemporary English Version © 1991, 1992, 1995 by American Bible Society. Used by permission.

Scripture quotations labeled Message are from The Message by Eugene H. Peterson, copyright © 1993, 1994, 1995, 2000, 2001, 2002. Used by permission of NavPress Publishing Group. All rights reserved.

Scripture quotations labeled NIV are from the Holy Bible, New International Version®. NIV®. Copyright © 1973, 1978, 1984, 2011 by Biblica, Inc.™ Used by permission of Zondervan. All rights reserved worldwide. www.zondervan.com

Scripture quotations labeled NLT are from the Holy Bible, New Living Translation, copyright © 1996, 2004, 2007 by Tyndale House Foundation. Used by permission of Tyndale House Publishers, Inc., Carol Stream, Illinois 60188. All rights reserved.

Scripture quotations labeled NRSV are from the New Revised Standard Version of the Bible, copyright © 1989, by the Division of Christian Education of the National Council of the Churches of Christ in the United States of America. Used by permission. All rights reserved.

Scripture quotations labeled TLB are from The Living Bible, copyright © 1971. Used by permission of Tyndale House Publishers, Inc., Wheaton, Illinois 60189. All rights reserved.

To protect the privacy of those who have shared their stories with the author, some details and names have been changed.

In keeping with biblical principles of creation stewardship, Baker Publishing Group advocates the responsible use of our natural resources. As a member of the Green Press Initiative, our company uses recycled paper when possible. The text paper of this book is composed in part of post-consumer waste.

green press INITIATIVE

14 15 16 17 18 19 20   7 6 5 4 3 2 1

Contents

Contents

Our Stories

The mission of Living Stones Associates is to help churches become healthier through integrated planning of ministries, staffing, facilities, and finances. The Living Stones team, now made up of ten consultants, has been partnering with churches throughout the United States and Canada for more than thirty years.

Every church the Living Stones Associates team has consulted with over the last thirty-plus years has been our teacher. Most of the stories in this book come from our experiences with these churches. Throughout the book, "we" typically refers to the Living Stones team, not just the authors.

When we tell where a church is located, we use the actual name of the church. When we name a church without a location, the name may be changed to protect privacy or the story may be a composite of several churches.

When one of us tells a personal story, the story is preceded by the author's name—*Eddy*, *Ray*, or *Skipp*. The end of these first-person stories is marked by a divider unless the first-person narrative continues to the end of the chapter.

1

The Possible Dream

Do you have a dream of what God could do in your church?

In 2004, Riverside Church in Big Lake, Minnesota, was at a crossroads. Over the past year, average attendance had grown by more than one hundred people to reach 670 in two services. Unless they added more space—and soon—they would in effect be posting a "No Vacancy" sign at a time when God was bringing them many spiritually hungry people.

Leaders had brainstormed several options:

- Sell their property, buy a larger site, and build.
- Buy land for expansion.
- Build a bigger worship center.
- Plant a sister church in a nearby community where some church families lived.
- Start a third service.

Riverside still owed $700,000 from their last building program, was spending 10 percent of the budget on mortgage payments, and had no building fund. Plus, the staff was stretched way too thin.

Without adding more staff soon, the church would quit growing and maybe even shrink.

Riverside had two options: stop growing or find creative ways to do more with less. So Riverside's leaders enlisted outside coaches to conduct an in-depth assessment of all their ministries, staffing, facilities, and finances to identify barriers to healthy growth and help them develop a plan to remove those barriers. Over the next two and a half years, they implemented that plan, and then repeated the process to update their plan.

Nine years later attendance has more than doubled, with more than two-thirds of Riverside's growth coming through evangelism, with hundreds of people each year saying yes to Christ and bringing their families and friends to come and see what they have experienced. As they say on TV, "These results are not typical."

Since 1980, Living Stones Associates[1] has partnered with hundreds of churches in the United States and Canada to do strategic planning for ministries, staffing, facilities, and finances. Every church we have worked with has become our teacher. Riverside, though, has been unique. Of all the churches we have partnered with, Riverside's leaders have most wholeheartedly embraced the more-with-less philosophy that guides our work. So, while Riverside's results are not typical, we return to their story often in this book because it shows what God can do when a church fully commits to more-with-less principles in every aspect of its life—more-with-less ministry, more-with-less staffing, more-with-less buildings, and more-with-less finances. Skipp, who has been on staff at Riverside through all these changes, tells the story.

> **Riverside had two options: stop growing or find creative ways to do more with less.**

More-with-Less Facilities

Skipp: Riverside's immediate barrier to growth was worship seating. Without more seats for worshipers, our attendance would hit a wall. But that wasn't our only facility challenge. Hallways and stairways were congested. Half our offices were on the main level and half were in the basement. The infant nursery was on one floor and the toddler nursery was on another. In many ways, the building made ministry harder rather than easier.

While we needed to increase worship capacity immediately, we had no money to build. In fact, a major building program would have inflicted even more damage on the church's already stretched finances. We needed a creative facility solution that was both quick and inexpensive. Which of the facility options we had been considering did we choose? None of them. Instead, we created a second worship venue, a video café, which immediately increased our worship seating capacity by one hundred seats per service.

Would it work? We didn't know, especially since the video café would not usually have live music. But to our delight, it was a hit from the start with worshipers of all ages making it their worship venue of choice. We later remodeled the video café to provide seating for 175. The video café gave Riverside breathing room to grow for six years before we needed to add a third service.

More-with-Less Finances

Riverside was bumping up against major barriers to growth in two key areas—facilities and staffing. Removing those barriers would cost money. Creating a video venue and remodeling the building to work better would cost a small fraction of what new construction would cost, but it would still take hundreds of thousands of dollars. Plus we urgently needed to pay off the church's debt so the 10 percent of our budget going to mortgage payments could be redirected to staffing.

In a three-year capital campaign, we raised 1.4 million dollars with sixty cents of each dollar going to the building project and the remainder going toward the debt. Over those three years, the church paid cash for its remodeling projects and technology upgrades and burned the mortgage. We have been debt-free ever since.

More-with-Less Staffing

As important as facility solutions were, and as exciting as it was to get out of debt, unless these steps had been combined with staffing for growth, Riverside's growth would have ground to a screeching halt. The 10 percent of the budget previously going to mortgage payments was redirected to staffing. This enabled the church to hire administrative support in several key areas, freeing up pastors and ministry directors to be more productive. Hiring our first executive pastor freed up senior pastor Tom Lundeen to focus on his strengths of teaching and leading while creating the infrastructure required to manage a growing staff.

More-with-Less Ministry

Remodeling did more than increase seating capacity; it also enhanced ministry. Families with young children loved the new nurseries, which were more modern, convenient, clean, comfortable, interactive, fun, and safe with a new secure check-in. Opening up rooms allowed the children's ministry to transition from small classes to a large group team-teaching model, increasing capacity and making ministry more effective. Changes to the foyer and nearby areas, along with a change in the Sunday schedule, made it possible to have a connections time between services so people leaving the first service could connect with those arriving for the second, and guests could connect with members over coffee and snacks. Creating an office suite brought the entire staff together, increasing efficiency and, more important, enhancing teamwork.

We had always had Sunday school classes for all ages, but our growth forced us to rethink our discipleship strategies. We began moving adult discipleship to home-based groups and small groups that met on the church campus during the week. That was a huge shift. Not only was it a smart use of space but the small groups have proven more effective for building community, changing lives, and caring for a growing church. On Sundays our students are encouraged to minister by serving on many of our teams—children's ministries, the tech team, ushers, greeters, the parking team, and our café team. This has been exciting! Today, all but a few classrooms are filled with excited children every Sunday morning.

Our biggest stride toward more-with-less ministry came six years ago. The church had two churchwide children's ministries—Sunday school and a Wednesday night program. While both had good leaders, they constantly struggled to recruit enough volunteers. Plus, the Wednesday program was not accomplishing one of its main purposes—reaching new families. Almost all the community kids coming on Wednesday already attended other churches.

As our children's ministry leaders realized how much duplication there was between our Sunday and Wednesday programs, they decided to combine the strongest elements of each to create a first-class Sunday ministry.

This was also a better fit for our ministry philosophy. We were asking our families to be at church two days a week, attend a small group, serve, and spend time reaching out to neighbors and friends. That was too much. Eliminating one meeting a week gave families time for small groups, service, and outreach.

> **Riverside's attendance has more than doubled, from 670 to about 1500. This has been accomplished without adding a single square foot to the facility that we thought was maxed out nine years ago.**

Since focusing on a single children's ministry, excellence has skyrocketed. When new families come, their kids beg their parents to come back. It's great to see kids so excited about church.

The Journey Continues

In the nine years since beginning our more-with-less journey, Riverside's average weekend attendance has more than doubled, from 670 to about 1500. This has all been accomplished without adding a single square foot to the facility that we thought was maxed out nine years ago. We are getting more use out of our facility than we ever thought possible.

This book explores the principles and strategies that have guided Riverside and many other churches to do more ministry with limited resources, even during financially challenging times. To benefit from these principles, your church's leaders will have to be open to exploring new ways of thinking about church, new ways of doing ministry that use limited resources more strategically. It will, at times, require leaving your comfort zone, but the payoff will be more fruitful ministry.

Part 1

More-with-Less Ministry

2

To Accomplish More, Do (and Spend) Less

Eddy: I once led a workshop on the topic, "When You Have More Slots Than Workers." It was standing room only. Before beginning my presentation, I asked each person to answer this question: "Why do you think churches so often have more slots than workers?"

One said, "People aren't committed." Another said, "The church is full of pew-sitters." All fifty-some people gave some version of the same answer: "We don't have enough workers."

When everyone had had their say, I announced: "I think you're all wrong! Nine times out of ten, the problem isn't too few workers, it's too many slots. If you came to learn how to recruit more workers, you may want to leave now and come back to this afternoon's workshop on recruiting. This workshop is on how to solve the problem of too many slots." No one left.

I witnessed a great example of too many slots at Stillmeadow Nazarene Church in York, Pennsylvania, some years ago. Like most churches we've worked with, the church had three church-wide weekly programs for children—Sunday school, children's church, and a huge Wednesday night program. To fully staff these programs that served about 150 children each week required ninety-one workers—or it would have if each worker worked every week. However, since there weren't ninety-one people willing to work every week, Carla, the children's ministry director, had sliced many of the slots into smaller pieces, asking people if they would help out once a month, or once every six weeks. Total slots to fill: 187. When I asked Carla, "Do you have 187 people who are called to work with children?" she just rolled her eyes. Eight positions were vacant and others were filled by people who were stretched way too thin.

> **Nine times out of ten, the problem isn't too few workers, it's too many slots.**

We suggested to Carla and her team that they come up with a way to do two children's ministry programs with excellence rather than trying to staff three programs. They decided to combine children's church with their Wednesday night program, using the best features of each, and hold it Wednesday night. On Sunday morning, rather than having Sunday school and two sessions of children's church, they changed their schedule so that they held two sessions of Sunday school during worship. They also switched from small classes to a large group team-teaching model that required fewer teachers and eliminated the need for department heads. After the restructure, Carla had not 187 slots to fill, but sixty, with every worker working every week. By June every position for the fall program was filled—a first—and all by people who were passionate about ministering to children!

The Price of Overprogramming

In the churches we work with, the too-many-slots syndrome is the rule, not the exception. Eighty to 90 percent of these churches are stretched so thin they are constantly scrambling for workers and are unable to do ministry with excellence. The result: workers burn out, those receiving ministry are shortchanged, and people are not free to serve where God has called them. While compromised ministry is the biggest casualty of overprogramming, there is a financial cost as well. It costs more to run three churchwide programs for children than to run two. It costs money to keep programs alive that have outlived their usefulness.

The financial cost of overprogramming is often hidden. Why? Because very little of the cost shows up in the program budget; it shows up mostly in the staff budget. A church accustomed to having certain programs often hires staff to keep them going, even when ministry impact would be greater with fewer programs done with greater excellence.

How We Got Here

Why has having too many programs become the rule rather than the exception? It goes something like this: God gives someone, or a handful of people, a vision for a new ministry. The new ministry is born with a flurry of excitement and good things happen. The next year another new ministry is born in much the same way. Good things happen. After a few years, the people who were called to start the first ministry move away from the community. Others step up to lead it. When those leaders step down, it proves hard to find willing new leaders. Eventually someone agrees to lead it, but more out of duty than passion. Meanwhile, two more ministries have started as God has planted vision in the hearts of new leaders.

> We are eager to give birth to new ministries, but are lousy at letting old ones die.

We are eager to give birth to new ministries, but are lousy at letting old ones die. We seem to feel that if we end a ministry program, we have failed. Our programs become sacred cows. Once when I was speaking to the leaders of a church about letting go of ministries that had served their purpose, the church historian stood and said, "I think we need to be careful when we talk about ending ministries. One hundred and ten years ago, God called a group of men to start one of our ministries. To end that ministry would be to disobey God."

Really? I felt like saying, "Are those men still here? Are they still leading that ministry?" One of the most common reasons for slot-filling is that when those whom God has called to lead a ministry have moved on and God has not called anyone else to step into their place, we recruit people to do it anyway.

To Be More Fruitful, Prune

Jesus's most focused teaching on how to be fruitful in ministry is found in John 15, the word picture of the vine and the branches. One of Jesus's secrets to fruitfulness in ministry is pruning. And it is the healthy branches that are pruned—the branches that produced last season's crop.

When branches are pruned, more of the life of the vine goes into producing the fruit. Without pruning, each year more and more of the sap of the vine goes into sustaining more and more branches and leaves, and each year the fruit is a bit smaller than it was last year.

Just as God prunes our lives, removing those good things that bore fruit in the previous season of our lives so all of our energy can be poured into new areas of growth, God does the same thing in the church. He calls us to new seasons of ministry, and at the same time no longer calls people to those ministries that bore fruit in previous seasons. When God is no longer calling people to lead a ministry, it is time to let go of it. It is pruning time. God wants to redirect the energy of those people into something new.

The birth of new ministry is a sign of life. But an equally important sign of health is being able to answer the question, "What ministry program have you ended this year?" If you can't think of one, you may have an overprogramming problem.

Streamlining Strategies

If God isn't calling someone to fill a slot, perhaps it shouldn't be filled. (There are exceptions: if no one feels called to clean the toilets, someone still needs to clean toilets.) When you have an empty slot and it seems that no one is being called to fill it, ask, "What is God saying to the church through this vacancy?"

Here are some possible answers.

1. *Prune.* Is it time to let go of "last season's" structures to which God is no longer calling people?
2. *Consolidate.* Can we combine programs with similar goals and participants? If we have two programs with the same purpose, we don't need them both.
3. *Restructure.* Can we adopt a different model that requires fewer workers, such as replacing solo teaching with large group team-teaching?
4. *Focus.* Can we find ways to do a few things with excellence rather than many things with mediocrity?
5. *Cap.* Would it be wise to limit enrollment in programs that tax available facilities and staff such as a daycare center or school?
6. *Prevent.* Can we avoid some overprogramming by making sure we only start new ministries when called, passionate leaders are in place? Be especially wary of starting a new program that calls for lots of volunteers, unless it is clear that lots of volunteers are called to the new ministry and that it will not compete with their present calls.
7. *Practice the two-hat principle.* Most core church leaders work in four, five, even six ongoing ministries. Whenever I ask these leaders how many of those ministries they are able to do with excellence, they usually say just one or two. They throw their hearts into their top one or two ministry priorities, but "fill slots" for the others. Encourage your leaders to wear no more than two ongoing ministry hats—one big hat (up to eight hours a week) and one small hat (up to two hours a

week). As you encourage them to pour all their energy into the one or two ministries for which they have the greatest passion, you can replace the unhealthy peer pressure to say yes to every request for help with positive peer pressure to focus on doing all ministry with excellence.[1] Of course, this will create empty slots. Those empty slots become clues to identifying needed pruning, restructuring, or consolidation.

Quit Trying So Hard

Several times after meeting with the leaders of a church, one of them has come up to us and said something like, "I was dreading today. I assumed you were going to tell us to do more, and I'm already doing so much I'm exhausted. I never dreamed you would encourage us to do less."

To accomplish more, do less. To bear more fruit, prune. To see God work more powerfully through you, listen and obey and trust, and quit trying so hard. In our workaholic culture, these words almost always come as a surprise, but they are also almost always welcome words for weary spiritual leaders.

Embracing this basic truth that our ministry is more effective not when we do more, but when we do fewer things with our whole hearts, is the first step in becoming a more-with-less church.

SELF-TEST:
Is Your Church Overprogrammed?

Answer *yes* or *no* to the following questions.

_____ 1. Is it an annual struggle to fill all the teacher/worker slots in your Christian education program?

_____ 2. Each year, are some people asked to serve primarily because the jobs need to be done rather than because they have a passion for that ministry?

_____ 3. Do you have two or more programs or regular services that serve similar purposes (such as children's Christian education, adult discipling, or family worship) that tend to compete with each other for participants' time or for leadership?

_____ 4. Does it take 75 percent or more of your available adult workers to fully staff all the ministries within the walls of the church, so that fewer than 25 percent of your people are working primarily in ministries outside the church walls?

_____ 5. Does your church have meetings, services, or programs that people attend more from habit or duty than because they are life-giving? (Clue: Do some of the old faithful complain about the lack of commitment of those who do not attend?)

_____ 6. Are leaders other than paid staff normally allowed (or perhaps even encouraged) to take on more than two ongoing ministry responsibilities—one major and one minor?

_____ 7. Has some major new ministry stalled in its development for lack of workers?

_____ 8. Have you recently overheard lay leaders say that church meetings and responsibilities are taking more time than they wished?

_____ 9. Do you have ministry programs in which it is easier to fill the "rank and file" spots than it is to fill the key leadership roles?

_____ 10. Do you often see signs of worker burnout—people feeling overworked, resigning from ministry positions earlier than they had planned to, or saying they need to take a break from ministry?

Bonus 1

_____ Does your church have a system in place to equip present and new members to identify not only spiritual gifts but also personal calls to ministry, and to help each one connect with a ministry that matches that call?

Bonus 2

_____ Does your church have a system in place that encourages and supports the birthing of new ministries when members identify calls to ministries not yet in existence?

Bonus 3

_____ In the past year, have you witnessed the birth of at least one new ministry program or ministry team that was not started by a church board or committee, but by a member in response to a vision God gave him or her?

Bonus 4

_____ In the past year, has your church deliberately ended at least one ministry program or regular meeting?

Bonus 5

_____ Has your church set a goal of eventually seeing about half of all adult members involved primarily in ministries outside the walls of the church?

Scoring: Score ten points for each _yes_ in response to questions 1 through 10. Then subtract twenty points for each _yes_ in response to the five bonus questions. Score _____

−100 to 0. Wow! A truly empowering church!

10 to 30. On track, but with growing room.

40 to 60. Time to get out the pruning shears.

70 to 100. You need to clarify your church's ministry vision so you can know where to prune.

3

To Reach More People, Disband Your Evangelism Committee

If all we know about a church is that it has an evangelism committee, we can be 90 percent sure it is not growing. New people are coming, of course, and attendance goes up and down, but chances are slim that the church is growing from year to year.

Why? Because if a church sees evangelism as the work of a committee, it doesn't see it as the responsibility of the whole church. Churches that are consistently growing through evangelism are outwardly focused. Evangelism is built into the DNA of almost everything they do.

A few churches have effective evangelism committees, but for the many that do not, a great next step is to replace the evangelism committee with a connections team.

Create a Connections Team

Some people in your church are passionate about making new people feel at home and helping them become part of the church family. We recommend that you identify these people and empower them to function as your connections team. They will be responsible for your greeting and ushering ministry, for follow-up, and for looking at your services and programs through the eyes of guests to suggest ways they can be more guest-friendly.

We suggest that you charge this ministry team with two goals: encourage them to experiment to find the best ways to achieve these goals, and then evaluate the results.

> **Connection 1:** Every Sunday guest who does not wish to be invisible will not leave the building until he or she has made at least one friend—a person who, when that guest returns a second time, will be looking forward to seeing the guest again and will greet him or her by name.

> **Connection 2:** Every first-time guest will be contacted within two to forty-eight hours of their first visit to the church with a doorstep visit, a phone call, or digitally, depending on what works best in the community.

According to Charles Arn, the average non-growing church assimilates one out of ten visitors into the congregation. Churches that are growing at the rate of 5 percent or more a year assimilate two in ten visitors into the congregation.[1] Having an effective connections team may be the single simplest thing you can do to increase the growth of your church.

Approach connections ministry as a calling, not as a chore that everyone has to take a turn at. It should be done by those who are most passionate about making people feel welcome.

Your connections team will have several subteams:

- *Greeters.* Depending on the size of your church, your greeting team may include most or all of the following: a lead greeter (in charge of the team for that service), door greeters, guest guides (who give tours of the church), welcome center greeters, and a scheduler.
- *Ushers.* Your ushers should be passionate about making people feel welcome and understand that this is their number-one job.

- *Parking lot attendants.* Attendants who enthusiastically welcome guests often make the strongest first impression on first-time guests.
- *Café/coffee team.* Your best opportunity to build relationships with guests on their first visit is during your connections time—a time after or between services where members and guests mingle over coffee and snacks. This team is responsible for preparing and serving food and drinks. Make sure to have kid-friendly items so families stick around.
- *Connections time hosts.* Your hosts are gifted people connectors who spend the connections time getting acquainted with guests and introducing guests to others who may have shared interests.[2]
- *Second connections team.* This team follows up with guests within two to forty-eight hours.

Charge this team with evaluating what you are now doing and sorting through which parts work well and which might be improved upon. Be prepared to try lots of things that don't work very well before finding what does work well.

Make Inviting Easy

Skipp: Most churches exhort their members to invite others; few give them the tools to make it easy. At Riverside, we give out yard signs for special events that people can display in their front yards. Our communications team provides e-vites, Facebook and web page links, and good old-fashioned paper invitations to give to family, friends, neighbors, and coworkers. And our people invite! From our connect card responses, we know that more than 80 percent of our guests come in response to a personal invitation from a friend or family member.

What do they invite people to? We have two kinds of events— *bridge-building* events and *invitational* events. The purpose of bridge-building events is to introduce people to Riverside. Some

of these events are onsite, such as our Car Care Day, our Sweetheart Banquet, and our Great Pumpkin Party that takes place the Friday before Halloween. Offsite events have included bus trips to major league baseball games and fun days at a water park. At bridge-building events, we don't make a gospel presentation. We do, though, pray over the food and enthusiastically tell our guests that if they are looking for a great church, we'd love for them to "come and see" what is going on at Riverside.

Invitational events involve both an invitation to the event and an invitation to say yes to Jesus. Riverside puts on three big all-church invitational events each year—Fall Kickoff, Christmas, and Easter. Our people are very active in inviting friends and neighbors to our Fall Kickoff using the tools we provide. Then during the Sundays in September we make sure that those who have accepted our first invitation to "come and see" are given the opportunity to accept our second invitation to say yes to Christ.

Our community is open to and engaged in artistic events. Twice a year, at Christmas and Easter, we capitalize on this by offering a dramatic musical production that tells a story relevant to people's lives. Between 2000 and 2500 people will attend these performances in a weekend. Since our auditorium seats only five hundred people at a time, we are constantly looking for ways to add more times and more seats. Our reputation for quality production makes inviting easy. Because our music, drama, and technical teams are made up of committed volunteers, we are able to offer tickets free of charge. The only thing we ask from the audience is that they complete a connect card.

WHAT ONE THING INFLUENCED YOU MOST TO COME?

____ My Friend, _____

__ Outdoor Banner__ Yard Sign   __ Invitation   ___ Newspaper

__ Facebook   __ Free Tickets   __ Church   __ Other_____

MY COMMENTS: _____
_____

BECAUSE EASTER MATTERS...

☐ **YES!** I am putting my trust in Jesus as my Leader.   ☐ **MAYBE** I am definitely thinking about it.

☐ I'm accepting your invitation to come back Easter Sunday.

NAME: _____ SPOUSE: _____

E/M: _____ PHONE: (____)_____

ADDRESS: _____ CITY: _____ ZIP: _____

I AM: ☐ An Adult   ☐ A Student (Gr. 6-12)   ☐ A Child (up thru Gr. 5)
I AM: ☐ Male   ☐ Female

In addition to the three all-church invitational events, our kids ministry team hosts a Mystery Night every couple of months, encouraging kids to invite their friends. The cost is three dollars for three hours of high-energy games, food, and fun activities. But if a child brings someone new, both the child and guest get in free.

Offer Free Samples

Video is a great tool for reaching new people. Posting videos of your services online gives people a great way to take a partial test drive of your church without even coming through the doors. Most of our first-time guests tell us they have already watched at least one service online, liked it, and decided to come check out Riverside.

Also, don't underestimate the power of video to keep attenders connected, encouraging them to take the next steps in their spiritual journeys. If the average attender only comes two out of four Sundays, that is barely enough to keep up with what is going on. If, however, you provide a way for them to watch a live stream of your service or even find a copy posted after the weekend, they can stay connected every week. Think of the difference that can make in people's lives and in your church!

Ask a Different Question

Church leaders often ask us, "How can we get more members?" (One even added, in all seriousness, "especially rich ones"!) Our response usually surprises them. We say, "We don't think that's a very good question. We think a much better question is, 'How can we become a healthier church?'" The most fundamental finding of the research behind Natural Church Development is that healthy churches tend to be growing churches.[3] In general, people are drawn to healthy churches, not to unhealthy churches.

> **Church leaders often ask us, "How can we get more members?" We say, "We don't think that's a very good question."**

While the suggested outreach strategies—forming a connections team, making inviting easy, and offering free samples—are all tried and proven, they are only effective if people visiting your church find a welcoming, life-giving, healthy church family. Likewise, if your church is extremely healthy, you won't be able to keep people away! Even if people aren't asked to tell others, they won't be able to keep from sharing the exciting things God is doing through their church and how it is changing their lives.

4

To Make More Disciples, "Teach" Less

Eddy: I have never before or since worked with a Christian education committee more passionate about its own mission. The members had invested hundreds of hours developing a detailed, carefully crafted list of all the Bible stories and concepts they wanted their children to learn in every quarter of Sunday school from kindergarten through sixth grade. Based on this list, they had written their own curriculum.

Their stated goals, however, said nothing about their children learning to love God, love others, care for creation, work for peace and justice, or share their faith. It's not that the committee didn't care about any of these things. Rather, they seemed to assume that if they just taught the Bible, life change would come automatically.

Jesus disagrees. When he said, "You are wrong, because you know neither the Scriptures nor the power of God" (Matt. 22:29), he was talking not to pagans, but to Bible scholars. These Pharisees could quote entire books of the Old Testament from memory. In fact, they probably could quote as much Scripture as Jesus could. Yet Jesus said they didn't know the Scriptures.

If Jesus visited many of our churches today, would his verdict be any better? You've probably read the polls about how Christians behave no better than everyone else on a wide range of ethical issues. Obviously, something about the way we have been teaching Scripture is terribly broken. We have often acted as if the Great Commission said, "teaching them *to know* everything I have commanded you" rather than "*to obey* everything I have commanded you" (Matt. 28:20 NIV). We have assumed that head knowledge leads to obedience. That may work sometimes, but evidently not often enough to make a dent in the polling data.

A Forgotten Part of the Gospel

In college I studied Christian education. I have forgotten most of what I heard in my Christian ed classes, but one session of a youth ministry class made a lasting impression. That day a guest lecturer, Norm Shoemaker, made an innocent-sounding observation that planted a subversive seed: "*Jesus's methods are just as much a part of the gospel as his message.*" How we make disciples, our speaker claimed, is just as critical as the message we teach them. That single sentence blew up most of what our prof had been teaching about Christian education.

> **Jesus's methods are just as much a part of the gospel as his message.**

The modern-day classic by Robert Coleman, *The Master Plan of Evangelism*, is based on a deceptively simple idea: if we want to learn how to make disciples, there is no better teacher than the master discipler himself. Coleman writes:

> At first glance it might even appear that Jesus had no plan. . . . It is so unassuming and silent that it is unnoticed by the hurried churchman. But when the realization of his controlling method finally dawns on the open mind of the disciple he will be amazed at its simplicity and wonder how he could have ever failed to see it before. Nevertheless, when his plan is reflected on, the basic philosophy is

so different from that of the modern church that its implications are nothing less than revolutionary.[1]

If we look to Jesus, and Paul as well, to learn how to make disciples, rather than unthinkingly going about it like we always have, we open ourselves to life-changing and church-transforming possibilities. Jesus defines disciple-making in Luke 6:40: "A disciple is not above his teacher, but everyone when he is fully trained will be like his teacher." Note: Jesus does not say a disciple, when fully trained, will know everything the teacher knows; he says the student will *be like* the teacher.

In school, the primary focus of teaching is communicating knowledge. The goal of disciple-making, though, is not information, but transformation. If Jesus's goal had been to teach his disciples as much knowledge as possible as fast as possible, he probably would have started a school. But he had a different goal, and so chose a different strategy: "He appointed twelve (whom he also named apostles) that they might be with him, and he might send them out" (Mark 3:14).

At first glance, that may look like a simple reporting of fact, but it's much more than that. It captures Jesus's discipling strategy in a single sentence. Jesus's purpose for his disciples was that they would *be like him*. So what did he do? He chose twelve to *be with him*. They would go where he went, sleep where he slept, watch as he healed, listen as he taught, ask him questions, and work alongside him.

Did this "with him" strategy work? When Peter and John were arrested for preaching and brought before the Sanhedrin, Luke describes the scene this way: "When they saw the courage of Peter and John and realized that they were unschooled, ordinary men, they were astonished and they took note that these men had been *with Jesus*" (Acts 4:13 NIV). Jesus chose twelve men to be *with him*. The only way the Sanhedrin could explain the actions of these *unschooled* men was that they had been *with Jesus*.

The Discipling Relationship

Who is the one person who has had the greatest positive influence in shaping your spiritual life? A parent? Grandparent? Teacher? Pastor? Spouse? Whoever it is, that person is the best example in your life of a discipler.

Drawing on behavioral science literature on modeling and identification, Christian education expert Larry Richards identifies several factors that enhance the discipling process. How many of these do you see at work in Jesus's relationship with his disciples? How many were (or are) at work in your relationship with your discipler?

Four Marks of a Disciple-Making Relationship

- The disciple needs frequent contact with the discipler over time, leading to an open, caring relationship between them.
- The disciple must observe the discipler in various settings and situations, giving the disciple opportunity to see into the heart of the discipler.
- The discipler's actions must be clear and consistent and line up with the church's values.
- The discipler needs to explain his or her lifestyle, with instruction accompanying shared experience.[2]

The need for explanation is essential, but notice it comes last. Consider how Jesus taught his disciples to pray. Did he sit them down around the campfire one evening after a day's traveling and say, "Okay, guys, tonight's Bible study is on prayer"? Did he put together a Prayer 101 seminar?

No, he waited until the disciples came to him and said, "Lord, teach us to pray." These men had been praying all their lives, so why did they ask? Because from living with and watching Jesus, they recognized an intimacy with the Father that they didn't have. They wanted to know how to pray like he did. And so they said, "Lord, teach us to pray."

The frequent contact, the warm and loving relationship, glimpses into Jesus's heart, time spent together in many settings and situations, the clarity and consistency of Jesus's values that aligned with Israel's mission and purpose—all these came first. When these prompted the disciples' questions, only then did Jesus explain how to pray.

Jesus lived it with them. They asked about it. He explained it.

If Jesus had merely wanted to teach them the words to what we call the Lord's Prayer, he could have done that in ten minutes. Opening their eyes to a new way of thinking about and practicing prayer took years.

Who, Me?

Well, you might say, that approach works fine for Jesus, but I'm not comfortable setting myself up as an example. Yet we find Paul using the same approach. "Be imitators of me," he wrote, "as I am of Christ" (1 Cor. 11:1). Knowing full well that he followed Christ's example imperfectly, how could Paul urge the Corinthians to follow his example? Larry Richards is helpful here.

> Intimate relationships in the church will reveal a lack of perfection! We will not be able to model perfectly, as Jesus did, the character that is to become ours. What then do believers model as they come to know one another in the Body's love relationship? We *model for one another the process of transformation.* We can afford to let ourselves be known as imperfect persons, for in revealing our imperfection we also reveal the ministry which the Holy Spirit is performing in working His progressive change![3]

To make disciples, we don't have to have arrived. We just have to be on the journey.

Making More and Better Disciples

To make more and better disciples, we will need to do less "teaching"—rely less on sermons, Sunday school lessons, and content-driven Bible studies. We will need to redirect much of that energy to creating intimate communities where it is safe for people to regularly do open-heart surgery, allowing the Spirit to change them. The heart of the discipleship process is not "Christian education," but the kind of life-transforming relationships that a Jewish rabbi had with his disciples, that Paul had with Timothy, that the early Christians of Jerusalem and Corinth had with each other in their house churches.

> **The heart of the discipleship process is not "Christian education," but the kind of life-transforming relationships that a Jewish rabbi had with his disciples.**

Larry Richards summarizes the education literature on this subject:

> What we seem to be discovering is that the formal school setting *itself* defines certain relationships and certain kinds of sharing (of ideas, not feelings) as appropriate, and thus rules out the kinds of relationships which are significant for discipling! This does not mean that adults or children and adults can not come together to learn. But it does imply that when they do come together, it is best *not* to define that situation as a "school." As long as teachers and learners perceive themselves to be in school, they will not develop the kinds of relationships or the kinds of sharing which are important for discipling!
>
> Strikingly, it seems that when we adopted from our culture the formal school approach to nurture, we in fact set up the conditions under which discipling and growth in likeness are least likely to take place![4]

As we recover Jesus's forgotten methods, at the heart of our disciple-making strategy will be relationships that embody the characteristics listed earlier—frequent contact, warm and loving relationships, heart transparency, spending time together in various life settings, and so on. Classes can supplement the life transformation that takes place in intimate community; they cannot replace it. Families, small groups, discipleship triads, mentoring relationships, house churches—these are the kinds of settings in which discipling relationships can thrive.

A Modest Proposal

When our team arrived at a Michigan church, the youth pastor eagerly took us to the basement that had been transformed into the coolest hangout space in town for students—a game room, an internet café, a concession stand, and a big meeting room. "We have 150 kids in here every Saturday for our Saturday Night Live program," he told us. It was impressive.

The next day when we met with him, we asked him, "How many adult volunteers do you have working with your youth?"

"Twenty-five," he said.

"How many of those know how to make disciples?"

He looked a bit sheepish and said, "Maybe five or six."

"And of the 150 youth who come on Saturday night, how many of them are integrated into the life of the congregation? How many worship with you on Sunday?"

"Fewer than ten."

"Bringing in a big crowd on Saturday night is great if it is a doorway into disciple-making relationships," we reminded him. "But don't forget: your call is not to get kids off the streets on Saturday night; your call is to make disciples."

A year later this youth pastor called us. "I confess that when you were here last year, what you said stung," he said. Then he went on to report his new numbers to us. He didn't mention how many students were showing up on Saturday night. But he did tell us that all twenty-five of his adult workers now knew how to make disciples, and he reported that twenty-five youth were now fully engaged in the life of the church and were growing spiritually. He had changed how he measured success.

Consider this modest proposal. Rather than measuring your success by counting how many people listen to sermons or Bible lessons, what if you tracked the number of people who are engaged in relationships that exhibit the four marks of a disciple-making relationship?

You will end up with fewer classes. You will need fewer classrooms. And you will see more lives and more relationships transformed.

——— Making Disciples Three at a Time ———

"I admit I stumbled onto a discovery; yet it has become one of the most amazing aha's of my pastoral ministry," writes Greg Ogden.[5] For many years he had championed one-on-one discipling—the Paul-Timothy model. Then came the experiment.

As his final project for his doctor of ministry program, Ogden was testing a discipleship curriculum he had written. At his adviser's suggestion, he experimented with the curriculum in three settings: one-on-one, a group of ten, and a group of three. While all three settings produced growth, to Ogden's surprise, the triad led to the greatest life change. "I did not anticipate the potency that would be unleashed in what I have since come to call a triad," he says. "It would forever change my understanding of the means that the Holy Spirit uses to transform people into Christ's image."[6]

Why Three?

How could adding just one person to the one-on-one model change the entire feel of what happened in the relationship, Ogden wondered. Here is what he has come to believe:

- When a third person is added, there is a shift from the discipler as focal point to the discipler as fellow participant.
- There is a shift from hierarchical to relational interaction.
- There is a shift from dialogue to dynamic interchange.
- There is a shift from limited input to wisdom in numbers.
- There is a shift from addition to multiplication.[7]

This last point needs to be unpacked. In theory, one-on-one discipling should lead to reproduction. Once someone is discipled, he or she disciples someone else. But Ogden admits that in practice, the reproduction rate is low. He now believes this is because one-on-one discipling relationships tend to be hierarchical, and hierarchy tends to create dependency. Those being mentored see themselves as receivers, not givers. Ogden observes, "As long as there is the sense that one person is over another by virtue of superior spiritual authority, however that is measured, few people will see themselves as qualified to disciple others."[8]

What Do Triads Do?

A triad is a group of three, usually all men or all women (same-gender groups tend to produce faster spiritual growth) who meet regularly to share life, encourage one another, pray for one another, and, optionally, to study.[9] Even when triads use curriculum, the study is not the group's primary focus; the focus is relationships. Ogden makes a compelling biblical case that it is relationship, not book learning, which drives the process of transforming discipleship.

Some triads meet weekly for lunch or breakfast. Moms with young children can meet at the park or at a home while they watch their kids play. Exercisers can walk together, sharing and praying as they walk. It is often better if a triad does not fill up a "prime time" slot such as an evening, as that stresses busy schedules. You're going to eat breakfast and lunch anyway. If you can meet over a meal, it costs you very little time.

"Fast Track" Small Groups

When churches ask us for help with small groups, we sometimes recommend they develop one or two prototype small groups, get outside training for small group leaders, identify a qualified person to be the small groups coordinator (paid or unpaid), and then, after several months, multiply the prototype small groups. Group leaders need a wide range of skills: facilitating meetings, leading worship, identifying and training apprentices, mentoring group members in evangelism, and so forth. Such leaders are actually pastors, and it's an exciting and high calling.

But growing that kind of small group culture throughout a church takes years. When a church needs small group help *right now* and it does not have leaders with the experience and passion to develop a traditional small group ministry, we now usually recommend that the church start with discipleship triads.

Why?

- *Starting triads is simple.* Pray about whom to invite, and then extend the invitation. You may want to give the person a copy of *Transforming Discipleship* by Greg Ogden, or this sidebar.

- *Triads don't require trained leaders.* By the time someone has come to three or four triad meetings, he knows enough to start another triad.

- *Triads need almost no administrative support.* A traditional churchwide small group ministry requires extensive administration and coaching from staff or a key volunteer. Triads are self-governing.

Synergy with Small Groups

Triads can be a powerful complement to traditional small groups. Most small groups need to build intentional outreach into their DNA. Why? Because Jesus calls us to go and make disciples. However, this sometimes limits intimacy. With the joining of every new member, the trust level of the group drops and must be rebuilt. During those times when there is less intimacy in my small group, my triad can meet my need for a place where it is safe to share deeply. It can keep me from placing unrealistic expectations on my small group.

Plus, if your triad members are from your small group, that creates a great synergy. When your small group meets, you are strengthening your triad relationships; when your triad meets, you are strengthening your small group. Far from competing with each other, your small group and triad build up one another.

If you are looking for intimate companions for your journey, or if your church needs a simple, powerful way to inject new life into your small group ministry, discipleship triads may be just what you're looking for.

5

To Empower for Ministry, Ax Committees

Eddy: St. Paul's Methodist in Wichita, Kansas, had a typical committee structure: a seventeen-member council, a finance committee (twelve members), trustees (seven), personnel (seven), stewardship (six), nurture ministries (six), and outreach (two). These all met monthly, and five other committees met as needed. There was nothing unusual about this structure, but for St. Paul's it was a problem. With an average worship attendance of seventy-nine, including children, and ninety-five committee and council positions to fill, almost every willing adult had to serve on multiple committees. All the usual complaints were common—too many meetings, boring meetings, meetings that ran late into the night, the struggle to recruit committee members, members who didn't participate, endless discussions without decisions, decisions that didn't get implemented, and power struggles.

If these meetings had all been delivering exciting, life-changing ministry, it might have felt like spending several nights a month in long, boring meetings was worth it. But they weren't. The church was in big trouble and, unless there was a major turnaround, it would die.

Over the next couple of years, the church's leaders did amazing work to restore unity, return focus to ministry, and begin building a healthy team culture. Hope and excitement returned. With the crisis past, I suggested they streamline their board and committees so people could spend more time doing ministry and less doing administration.

It was a year or so before I visited the church again. When someone told me how, with the guidance of their district super-intendent, they had shrunk their council, eliminated some committees, and downsized and combined others, my jaw must have dropped. She looked puzzled. "But you said to spend less time on administration and more time on ministry. We just did what you told us," she said.

> **Streamline boards and committees to spend less time doing administration and more time doing ministry.**

Indeed they had—and they had succeeded beyond anything I had imagined. Today the church council has seven members, not seventeen. Instead of having a twelve-member finance committee and seven-member trustee committee, one council member serves as finance chair and another as trustee chair. When the council considers trustee or finance committee decisions, those chairs lead those parts of the meeting. The personnel committee has shrunk from seven to five. Other committees have been disbanded, combined, or replaced by ministry teams.

While this exact structure wouldn't work for most churches, any church with a board and committee structure can benefit from living by this rule: *streamline boards and committees to spend less time doing administration and more time doing ministry.*

Our Love-Hate Relationship with Committees

We smile at the old wisecrack, "For God so loved the world that God didn't send a committee." Yet in many churches, committees are sacred cows. At one church, fewer than half the committee members came to the meetings, yet it had not occurred to anyone to shrink committees of twelve or fourteen to the five or six who actually attended. Why not? Because being on a committee was how you knew you belonged in that church, even if you had no intention of participating. Another church's welcome brochure encouraged first-time visitors to get involved by—you guessed it—joining a committee.

One church's bylaws called for each administrative committee to have three to nine members. They all had nine. Why? So more people would feel included. We've seen finance committees of fourteen or fifteen; church boards of over fifty!

At one fairly typical church we asked the leaders to write down how many hours a month they spent in meetings hearing and giving reports (or writing reports in preparation) and discussing ministry. Then we asked them to write down how many hours a month they spent actually *doing* the ministry their boards or committees oversaw. On average, they spent three to four hours *talking about* their ministries for every hour they spent *doing* them.

By expecting most of our leaders to serve on boards and committees, we are asking many people who don't have the gift of administration to do administration. They end up wasting lots of time and suffering considerable frustration, while ministries are hobbled by poor management systems. Is it any wonder so many leaders are discouraged by how little ministry fruit they are seeing from their huge investment of time?

There is a reason the Holy Spirit only gives the gift of administration to a few: it only takes a handful of gifted administrators to support a host of people doing ministry.

Streamlining administration to maximize ministry requires a paradigm change. We must begin by recognizing that the more-the-merrier, bigger-is-better approach to boards and committees that most of us take for granted doesn't enhance ministry but rather makes it slower, more complicated, and more frustrating. Then we must catch a vision of a new, more empowering way to do ministry together and begin the transition from Ministry 1.0 (the old way) to Ministry 2.0 (the new way).

Committees vs. Teams

In envisioning a better way, a good place to start is with the difference between committees and ministry teams. While some boards and committees function as healthy teams, it's rare. Here are the key differences:

Committees vs. Ministry Teams

Committees	Ministry Teams
Committees may include people not doing the ministry who are making decisions about other people's ministries.	Teams are made up only of people doing the ministry, making decisions about their own ministry.
Members serve based on availability and willingness.	Members serve based on call.
Leaders work with those assigned or elected to the committee.	Ideally, the team leader has final say about who is and is not on the team.
Committees often have little authority to change ministry strategy.	Teams can adopt any strategy consistent with the church's vision and values.
Trust and transparency are often low. Healthy conflict may be rare.	Trust is high. It is safe to disagree. Vigorous, creative conflict is normal.

A Christian education committee, for example, may include people not actually involved in working with children or youth. The committee is basically charged with "keeping the programs staffed and running." This includes selecting curriculum and recruiting teachers. Changes to the basic structure of the Christian education program are typically beyond the committee's authority. This approach often results in teachers using curriculum they find frustrating, feeling trapped by exasperating structures, and experiencing chronic recruiting struggles.

With the team approach, the Christian education committee is replaced by a children's ministry team made up of those most passionate about ministry with children, a youth ministry team made up of those most passionate about discipling youth, and perhaps an adult discipleship team made up of the most strategic adult small group leaders. Not every children's worker or youth worker is on the ministry teams, only the most passionate leaders who are gifted in planning. Every team member is immersed in the ministry. If the team wishes to draw on the expertise of others not personally involved in the ministry, they can enlist the help of mentors or trainers, but they don't join the team.

At St. Paul's Methodist, everyone recognized that the worship committee, mired in conflict, wasn't working. Their solution? They disbanded the worship committee and replaced it with a worship planning team made up of the pastor and others responsible for planning and leading worship.

Servant Administrators

In the world, administration is identified with control. Jesus said, "You know that the rulers of the Gentiles lord it over them, and their great ones exercise authority over them. It shall not be so among you. But whoever would be great among you must be your servant" (Matt. 20:25–26). There is only one place in Scripture where spiritual gifts are ranked: "First apostles, second prophets, third teachers" and so on (1 Cor. 12:28ff.). Administration, interestingly, comes near the end of the list. This is not, of course, because administration is unimportant. It is essential for the healthy functioning of the body of Christ, and often undervalued. Rather, it is because in the church, those with the gift of administration are not to exercise top-down authority over others but are instead to nurture an environment where the ministries of others can thrive. In a healthy church, administrators are more like gardeners than CEOs. They measure success not by their personal achievements but rather by the fruitfulness of the ministry teams they support.

The Five Kinds of Teams

To see how administrators can empower ministry in a team-based church, it helps to understand the five kinds of teams.[1]

- *Core ministry teams* do the ministries that are considered essential to the church's identity. While each church must define which ministries are core, some common core ministry teams are worship, children's ministry, youth ministry, adult discipleship, and connections. Some core teams will have subteams. For example, a tech team may be a subteam of the worship team. The connections team may have subteams of greeters, hosts, ushers, and those who follow up with guests.

- *Edge ministry teams* are usually grassroots teams that are not essential to the church's identity (if they disappeared, the church would still be the same church) but that grow out of a call God has given to the team members. A nursing home outreach, Mothers of Preschoolers (MOPS), a food pantry, and a motorcycle ministry would in most churches be considered edge ministries. Because edge ministries are not essential to the church's identity, they have more freedom to fail and can experiment more.

- *The staff team*, which may include both paid and unpaid ministry leaders, leads the implementation of the church's vision through ministry teams. Core and edge ministry teams are coached, directly or indirectly, by staff team members, and they report through the staff. (See chapter 11 for more on the staff team.)

- *The governing board* defines and safeguards the values and vision of the church, adopts policies, oversees and evaluates the work of the senior pastor, and with the staff nurtures an environment that empowers ministry teams to thrive.

- *Administrative support teams* (or committees) assist the governing board with specific aspects of their work, not to control but to support and empower ministry teams. Common administrative support teams are finance, facilities, personnel, and nominations.

Streamlining Tips

The goal of spending less time on administration and more time on ministry can be framed as streamlining the functions of the governing board and administrative support teams (committees) while maximizing the time and energy invested in the ministry teams. Here are a few guidelines for streamlining your board and administrative support teams.

- If at all practical, limit teams to a maximum of seven or eight people. A board or committee becomes less efficient with each person added beyond seven.

- If you have a representative board (most members represent a program or constituency), consider restructuring so that ministries report to the staff, not the board.

- Get your board out of the management business. Make your staff team responsible for managing the day-to-day ministries of the church. Empower ministry teams to make strategy decisions for their own ministries so long as they are within the values and vision defined by your board.[2]

- Eliminate any committees (administrative support teams) whose jobs can be handled more efficiently either by the board or the staff. One church hired an administrator whose responsibilities included contracting for building repairs. However, the facility committee continued to meet and vote on repairs—*after* contractors had completed them. Obviously, the church had outgrown its facility team.

- If personnel or finance teams are needed, consider limiting them to three people. In a church that has fully transitioned to policy governance (which is what we are describing here), the staff team prepares the budget. The finance team is responsible only for financial policies, procedures, and oversight to ensure financial integrity.

- Meet only when necessary. Most administrative support teams don't need to meet monthly. If a meeting is scheduled but there is just one agenda item that can be handled by email, cancel the meeting. When a church has fully transitioned to policy governance, even its governing board may only need to meet every two or three months.

- Remember that when administrative groups meet less often, they are more likely to stay focused on governance and supporting ministry teams and will be less tempted to stray into management, which is the assignment of the staff team.

- Do not nominate people who tend to be controlling to serve on your governing board or administrative support teams. Remember, biblical administrators are not called to control but to support the ministries of others. Nominate humble people who are passionate about empowering others, not about getting their way.

- If you use a nominating committee, it is the most important committee in your church. Get this committee right and you will probably have an effective board. Get it wrong and your board and committees will come back to bite you. Appoint spiritually mature people with the gift of administration to fill about half the slots on this committee. People with this gift have a special ability to discern which people will best serve in which roles.

Enlisting a few gifted servant administrators to create and nurture a culture that empowers ministry is the first half of correcting the imbalance between administration and ministry. The next chapter explores the second half—equipping and empowering people to fulfill their callings through teams.

6

To Multiply Leadership, Recruit Fewer Leaders

When we ask volunteer leaders what part of their work they find most draining, the most common answer is "recruiting." A pastor of a church of six hundred in West Virginia shook his head, frustrated that "God just hasn't given us very many teachers." Every year thousands of nominating committees scramble to find people to serve on boards and committees. There just aren't enough people able and willing to fill all the slots.

There are two reasons for this "more slots than workers" dilemma. First, most churches are overprogrammed. They have too many slots. The solution is to reduce the number of slots using the strategies described in chapter 2.

Second, most churches try to fill leadership roles by *recruiting readymade leaders*. Like this West Virginia pastor, they assume that if God isn't sending the church enough readymade leaders, all they can do is pray and wait. What they miss is that the most effective core strategy for filling leadership roles is not recruiting leaders but growing leaders. Ephesians 4:12 doesn't tell us to "*recruit* the saints to do the work of ministry," but rather to "*equip* the saints for the work of ministry." All too often, while saying that "leaders are made, not born," we keep looking for readymade leaders for our ministries.

From Recruiting Leaders to Growing Leaders

Eddy: When I came to Hilltop Urban Church in Wichita, Kansas, a multiethnic congregation in a poor neighborhood, all our programs were led by educated, middle-class people who had come from our suburban partner churches. Suburban people led the ministries; neighborhood people received ministry. While the pastor was passionate about raising up indigenous leaders, he wasn't sure how to go about it.

The Hilltop neighborhood is where people in Wichita land when they hit bottom. If they get back on their feet, most move out. Broken homes, addictions, teen pregnancy, domestic abuse, illiteracy, and jail time are common. Not surprisingly, almost none of the neighborhood people who attended the church had ever led ministries.

> The most effective core strategy for filling leadership roles is not recruiting leaders but growing leaders.

Today, one of the things Hilltop is best at is growing homegrown leaders. Most of our ministry team members and small group leaders are neighborhood people who five years ago could not have imagined they would ever be able to lead anything. Most of our "recruited" leaders from suburban partner churches have now returned to their home churches, having successfully planted an urban church.

If it can happen in Hilltop, it can happen anywhere.

How did a church that had always relied on recruiting readymade leaders develop a culture of growing leaders from within?

Leadership Incubators

Over four years, Hilltop transitioned all of our ministries from a traditional program approach where program leaders recruit people to fill ministry slots and oversee the volunteers (for example, a Sunday school superintendent recruiting teachers) to a team approach where those called to the ministry plan and do it together.

Team vs. Working Group

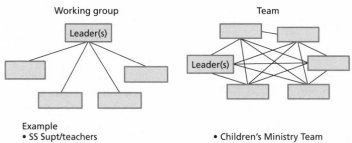

Example
• SS Supt/teachers   • Children's Ministry Team

This is not to say that all ministry should happen in teams. When a job can be done just as well by people working individually, it may not be worth taking the extra time and energy to build a team. Even great teams do parts of their work in working group (or "single-leader group") mode.[1]

But when you want to get all the best ideas on the table, when you want people's brainstorming to trigger new ideas, when you want to fully engage the quieter group members in the creative process, when you need complementary gifts feeding off of each other, when you want the contagious energy that comes from working arm in arm with people who share your passion—nothing less than a team will do.

The creativity unleashed and the results achieved by a healthy team can be incredible. Even more incredible, though, is the power of team ministry to grow leaders. A person with almost no confidence who has never led anything can join a team and within two or three years be a confident, effective leader. While a team's ministry may impact many lives, often the transformation in the lives of team members is even greater.

Ministry teams are leadership incubators. At Hilltop we have discovered that inviting people to join healthy teams is by far our most effective leadership development strategy. Everything else we do to grow leaders supplements this core strategy.

The Care and Feeding of Teams

If a church announces, "We are transitioning to a ministry team approach," a couple of things typically happen. A few teams thrive because they have leaders who are gifted at team building. Some committees are renamed "teams" but continue to operate just as they did before. Some working groups may be renamed "teams" but continue to operate as they always have. The church ends up with pockets of team ministry, but something far less than a team culture.

> **Inviting people to join healthy teams is by far our most effective leadership development strategy.**

Transitioning all of a church's ministries to a team culture takes several years, but, of course, time alone doesn't produce teams. It also takes training and coaching. To create and maintain a team culture in your church, every team leader must have a coach who regularly meets with the team leader, who is on call when the team leader feels stuck or overwhelmed, and who is passionate about growing leaders. Of course, providing intensive coaching for every ministry team and small group will require most churches to reprioritize staff responsibilities and sometimes hire staff with different skills.[2]

Talent Scouts

A common mistake is *recruiting* people to lead without *equipping* them to lead. When we ask inexperienced people to lead and we offer little coaching support, we set them up for frustration and failure. This doesn't mean we don't need to recruit. It does mean that often we will not be recruiting leaders but rather future leaders. We will always be on the lookout for people we can encourage to join a team. In a church with a culture of raising up homegrown leaders, our staff members, ministry leaders, and small group leaders are all talent scouts. They are constantly wondering, *What gifts and passions does this person have? Where would be a good place for him or her to begin serving?*

While some people will volunteer, about half will need someone to tap them on the shoulder and invite them to serve. Why? Usually because they lack confidence. It can make all the difference when a talent scout says something like, "I noticed how wonderful you are at making new people feel welcome. Would you be willing to pray about joining our connections team? I think that ministry would be a great match for your gifts."

Investing in Equipping

For the past thirteen years, we have been asking the churches we work with to report how much money they invest in leadership development. We looked to see if there was any relationship between the amount of money invested in equipping and the church's health or growth. What we found surprised us.

We found that the amount churches spend on continuing education for paid staff had no measurable correlation to church health or growth. Why is that? A possible explanation is that those churches that spend the most for pastors' continuing education tend to use much of that money for schooling, sometimes advanced degree programs. While advanced degree programs often open doors for career advancement for pastors, most churches suffer from the pastors' unavailability during the program. Also, only about 10 percent of the skills needed to effectively lead a congregation can be learned in the classroom. In fact, as counterintuitive as this may seem, two major research projects show that the more years of formal education a senior pastor has, the less likely the church is to be a healthy, growing church.[3] This is not to say that there is no place for academic training of pastors. It is to say that when we make schooling central to pastoral training, we neglect more critical equipping strategies and so get a poor return on investment.

More-with-Less Leadership Development

Investing just 2 percent of your church's total spending for leadership development can make a huge difference in creating an equipping culture in your church. Where can you strategically invest to develop your unpaid ministry leaders?

1. *A leadership development budget for each ministry team.* Each year when ministry team leaders submit their budget requests, we suggest that the first line item in that budget be leadership development. A worship team might, for example, bring in a coach for a Saturday worship arts workshop. The coach could attend a rehearsal and offer feedback, work with the tech team, and have coaching sessions with the worship team leaders. The children's ministry team might go to a workshop together. The elder team might bring in an outside coach to facilitate the elder retreat, guiding strategic planning, facilitating conflict resolution, or helping them navigate change. We generally recommend that every ministry team have a one-day or weekend retreat each year that includes a training component. This budget line pays for that retreat.

2. *An annual "pilgrimage."* One of the most powerful more-with-less training strategies is for a group of ministry leaders and team members to go on a pilgrimage each year. The staff and board identify the ministry area where the church most needs to grow during that year, and anywhere from half a dozen to fifty of your people, depending on the size of your church and the ministry area, travel together to a training event or to immerse themselves in the life of another church for a weekend. One year you might take all your worship teams to a worship conference. Another year your small group leaders might go to a small groups conference. If you are exploring launching another campus, some of your most strategic leaders might visit several multisite churches to experience how they do it and pick the staff members' brains about what worked, what didn't work, and what they will do differently the next time they launch a new campus.

The reason for group pilgrimages is not just to gather information. One person could do that. It is so you can all, together, experience a different way of doing church through immersion in a different ministry culture. Also, traveling together gives people focused time to share what they are seeing and begin processing what might and might not work in your church. Your leaders start growing a *shared vision* of new ways to do ministry. During a weekend pilgrimage, leaders can make a major paradigm shift that might otherwise take years.

3. *Leadership community meetings.* When we ask pastors about leadership development, they often talk first about classes. While making classes the heart of your leadership development is a formula for ineffectiveness (relational strategies such as team involvement, apprenticeship, and pilgrimages are primary), there is a time for "instruction accompanying shared experience."[4] It can be valuable to bring all of your ministry team leaders and members together for vision casting, discussing the church's future, and training. While some churches do this monthly, in most churches every two or three months is probably enough. Never have a leadership community meeting just to have a meeting. Make sure it is a high-value time, that people leave feeling like they got a great return on the time they invested. Otherwise they won't keep coming back. A Saturday morning or Sunday evening format, starting with a meal and meeting for three hours or so, works well. The training piece can be led by staff, members of the congregation, or outside coaches. If you do this with excellence, it can be a powerful supplement to your core methods of leadership development.

Recruit Fewer Leaders

As long as you fill leadership roles primarily by recruiting, you will constantly struggle with having more slots than leaders. Developing a churchwide culture of leadership development, on the other hand, creates the potential for long-term healthy growth. There will still be times when you need to recruit staff from outside, although increasingly you will be hiring homegrown staff. While you will still recruit experienced volunteers, you will be recruiting even more emerging leaders.

As you transform your church into a farm system for "equipping the saints for the work of ministry," you multiply leadership and, along with it, your church's potential for ministry in your community and around the world.

7

To Improve Health,
Stir Up Conflict

"Relational conflict is what the Bible calls sin," reads a discipling manual we came across at one church. That says it pretty straight, doesn't it? But there's a basic problem with this perspective: it's wrong. While, of course, sin does breed some conflicts, other conflicts grow out of nothing more sinister than differences in experience or personality or even spiritual gifts.

Not all conflict is bad. Much tension is life-giving—inviting us to grow, learn, or develop intimacy. Churches that habitually run from conflict (and there are lots of them) don't just miss out on these growth opportunities; they end up sick.

Chances are, in your church you've witnessed firsthand some of the crippling consequences of conflict avoidance.

Making Lowest-Common-Denominator Decisions

As one church launched a comprehensive planning process, a member rose and addressed the consultant: "One thing you need to know about this church is that we are very careful to not offend anyone." Translation: "Don't you dare rock the boat! We don't want to make any decision that anyone doesn't like."

Down this path lies paralysis. Doing nothing until everyone likes it gives the most negative members of the congregation veto power. It ensures that new and exciting changes will be rare, and it practically guarantees that many of the most passionate, outreach-oriented members of your congregation will leave. Why? Because by empowering those slowest to embrace change, you are disempowering your most creative leaders. Many of them will find another church that supports them in pursuing the vision for ministry God has given them.

> **Churches that run from conflict end up sick.**

No church can keep everybody happy. Some people are going to leave. But you can choose which group you will lose—your most entrepreneurial, visionary leaders, or those most fearful of change.

One Detroit pastor got this right. During a time of vision work that released great energy in the congregation, one member—a major giver—announced that if the church installed theater lighting in the sanctuary for a proposed ministry, he would leave. The pastor's answer: "We'll hate to see you go, but we can't hold up the rest of the congregation for one person." That church is well on its way to getting unstuck.

Settling for Shallow Relationships

Conflict is essential to developing intimacy. Until people have gone through conflict together and come out on the other side, the relationship is untested. Working through differences constructively forges deep bonds of trust.

In the life cycle of a small group, for example, the first stage of group life is the honeymoon. This is followed by a conflict stage, through which the group must pass to reach the third stage—community. If a group spends too long in the honeymoon stage—staying at the level of pleasant, superficial acquaintance—a wise group leader will prod the group to work through conflict people have been avoiding so the group can move ahead on the path toward mature community.

In the same way, the strongest marriages are those where the partners have battled their way through many tough issues to achieve a hard-won mutual trust. These husbands and wives know that more challenges will come, but that doesn't scare them. They know they can work through them together and be stronger for it, because they've done it before.

> **Conflict is essential to developing intimacy.**

Sinking into Irrelevance

The pace of change in our culture keeps accelerating. This means that although the gospel never changes, our ministry style must constantly change to connect with a rapidly changing society. If we don't, we become culturally irrelevant.

When a congregation's leaders commit to cultural relevance, it pushes many of us beyond our comfort zones. Christians passionate about reaching out will often clash with those more concerned with their own comfort. Between "what I feel most comfortable with" and "the most effective way to fulfill our mission" often stretches a wide chasm.

Pat Kiefert, president of Church Innovations Institute, describes one finding of a congregational study done at Emory University by Nancy Ammerman:

> Every congregation that successfully adapted and flourished in a changing community had a substantial church fight. Those that chose to avoid conflict at all costs failed to flourish. No exceptions.
>
> Understand: There were no, I repeat, no exceptions.[1]

Pretending Differences Don't Exist

A committee member complained to her pastor about a long-standing committee policy that was causing problems. But when the committee discussed the policy at its next meeting, she kept quiet, insecure about expressing disagreement. So the other committee members still didn't know about the problem and ministry suffered.

Proverbs 27:17 says, "Iron sharpens iron, and one person sharpens the wits of another" (NRSV). When people sidestep working through differences, the iron never gets very sharp, working relationships remain strained, and the group tends to make poor decisions. In a healthy church, people know how to disagree without being disagreeable.

Being Complacent about Complacency

Eddy: I was having breakfast with several members of a church council who were considering launching a strategic planning process in their church. At the end of the meal, one man asked, "How can we convince our people we need this when they are so content with the way things are?" I knew this was a church that prized keeping the peace above almost everything else, so I suspect my answer shocked them.

"One of the most important responsibilities of church leadership," I said, "is to create tension. And you do that by making your people highly conscious of the gap between the way the church is and how God wants it to be. Make your people so aware of the something more that God is calling them to be that they can no longer be content with the way things are."

In a complacent church, it is the responsibility of the leaders to overcome their natural inclinations to keep the peace and instead disturb the peace.

Avoiding the Hard Work of Correcting Sin

Conflict-avoidant churches often empower the most divisive members to wreak havoc. Other members may quietly complain about the bullies, but rarely do they acknowledge that such people are committing a grievous sin and that the church is responsible to God to discipline them.

Why are we so slow to confront people who are damaging the church? Well, we know it's going to hurt, and most of us don't enjoy inflicting pain. And we may not relish the prospect of arousing the offender's anger. But perhaps a deeper reason is that the New Testament instructions for correcting one another are designed to be lived out in intimate community, and most of our churches today have much more the feel of institution than of community. Spiritual correction doesn't work well outside of intimate relationship, no matter how well-intended.

But, in spite of the challenges, for the church to be healthy we must find ways to give and receive correction.

Life-Giving Conflict

To be healthy, your church needs conflict.

- Every church has defining moments when it must choose between being true to its mission and pleasing people. Obeying God must always trump trying to keep everybody happy.

- The church cannot fulfill its destiny apart from becoming an intimate community, and successfully working through conflict, again and again, is essential to building community.

- All progress requires change, and all change brings some level of conflict. Working through the conflicts that come with constantly updating ministry will always be part of the cost of ministering effectively in a changing world.

- No ministry team can thrive while sweeping important differences under the rug. To draw out the best in people, the church must offer safe places where everyone knows that differing perspectives are not only tolerated but sincerely valued.

- When a church is complacent, the leaders are responsible for "disturbing the peace" by spotlighting the gap between what is and what needs to be until the members become so uncomfortable that they feel compelled to change.

- Finally, when conflict is fueled by sin, the church must respond graciously and firmly, speaking the truth in love, to restore the one who is sinning and to protect and heal the church from the damage caused by the sin.

One translation of Acts 4:32 says that the believers in the Jerusalem church "all felt the same way about everything" (CEV). That is far from true. The New Testament church consisted of diverse people who often disagreed, sometimes passionately. What Acts 4:32 really says is that the believers were "of one heart and soul." Their love for each other and their shared purpose inspired them to work through potentially explosive disagreements while respecting each other's differences, coming up with creative win-win solutions that embodied kingdom values. (See, for example, Acts 6 and 15.)

Such conflict is not the enemy. In fact, it is an absolutely essential element in the day-to-day rhythm of life in every healthy church.

May your church be blessed with many life-giving conflicts—and the grace to grow through every one of them.

SELF-TEST:
Working through Unhealthy Conflict

BY MIKE HARE AND EDDY HALL

While healthy conflict is essential to unleashing creativity, unhealthy conflicts must be confronted. Many conflicts can be resolved quickly and easily. Some require the decisive intervention of the church leadership. In other cases, the church will need to ask for outside help to avoid serious, long-term damage to the church. To determine which category your church's conflict falls into, answer the following ten questions *yes*, *no*, or *maybe*.

_____ 1. Do some people hold back from giving their honest views because they feel that others do not want to hear what they have to say, or for fear of being attacked?

_____ 2. Is conflict hindering the church's ability to make unified decisions on important issues?

_____ 3. Is bad behavior—such as name calling, gossiping, showing disrespect to leaders, intimidation, quarreling, disrupting meetings, lying, insubordination, attributing negative motives to others, etc.—being allowed to continue without people being held accountable for their behavior?

_____ 4. Is conflict damaging the congregation's witness in the community?

_____ 5. If you answered *yes* to question 2, 3, or 4, has the church's leadership defined a process for addressing the conflict? Is that plan being diligently implemented?

_____ 6. Has there been clear progress toward resolving the conflict during the past four months?

_____ 7. Is the lead pastor perceived as being so identified with divisive issues that he or she cannot be effective as a neutral facilitator?

_____ 8. Do at least 20 percent of your leaders consider the situation serious and urgent?

_____ 9. Has the pain of *not* doing the hard work of change become greater than the pain of doing the hard work of change?

_____ 10. Are your leaders committed to understanding the root causes of the conflict and dealing with them to restore health rather than just "putting out the fires"?

Interpreting Your Answers

Question 1 describes conflict avoidance. Most churches have a culture of conflict avoidance—sweeping conflict under the rug in hopes that it will take care of itself. While some minor conflicts do go away on their own, a pattern of conflict avoidance eventually leads to volcanic eruptions.

Churches that ignore conflict end up being bitten by it. In a healthy church the leaders are trained to "mine for conflict," to make healthy, vigorous conflict a part of every decision-making process.

For Question 1, the correct answer is *yes.* In every church, *some* people will feel nervous about expressing their views. This is why, in the healthiest churches, leaders will work to create safety for those who are afraid to share their thoughts and will reward people for saying difficult things even if they disagree with their views.

An answer of *no* suggests a lack of awareness of the fear of conflict that exists to some degree in every church. Without this awareness, the church will not be proactive in training leaders to facilitate healthy conflict.

Questions 2 through 4 identify conflict that is damaging the church. If you answered *yes* to one or more of these questions, your situation demands a prompt, decisive response.

Questions 5 and 6 gauge the church leadership's response to damaging conflict. If you answered *yes* to both questions, you are probably well on your way to resolution. If a significant conflict has festered for more than four months without clear progress, it may be time to consider seeking outside help.

Question 7 is a dead giveaway that outside help is needed. In minor conflicts, the pastor can often mediate. When a congregation is divided, however, the senior pastor usually becomes identified with one side. Even if the pastor has not contributed to the conflict, if all parties do not perceive the pastor as neutral, he or she is not in a position to facilitate resolution. This is true even when the pastor is a trained professional mediator.

Questions 8 through 10 show whether a church is ready to accept outside help. Just because a church *needs* outside help doesn't mean it is *ready* for it. A lot of people need marriage counseling, but if they don't want marriage counseling, they are not likely to benefit from it.

For a church to be ready to receive outside help, a critical mass of the church's leaders must be convinced that the situation is serious and urgent. We have worked with churches in crisis whose pastors or board members didn't believe they were in crisis. We couldn't help those churches. A church is only ready to do the hard work of dealing with the root causes of conflict when the pain of not changing has become greater than the pain of changing.

Finally, some people seek counseling when their pain becomes unbearable, but as soon as the pain lets up they quit going—without dealing with the root issues. Some churches do the same thing. Inviting outside help gives the church a rare opportunity to gain insight into the church's core health and make changes that can enhance the church's effectiveness for the next decade. When a church abandons the process as soon as the pain subsides, it wastes an amazing opportunity for transformation.

Working through conflict offers a church a great opportunity to make core changes that can take effectiveness to a new level. In a crisis, people are open to making changes they would not consider at other times. Wise leaders will make the most of the strategic opportunities created by seasons of conflict.

8

To Increase Unity, Throw Out Your Vision Statement

It was an incredible weekend. At a gorgeous mountaintop retreat, Pastor Jerry and the elders of Crossroads took forty-eight hours to pray, dream about what God had in store for their church, and then draft a vision statement. They didn't need to revisit their mission statement. It was timeless—drawing mainly on the Great Commission and the Great Commandment. But vision, well that was a different matter.

Over the past couple of years it had become obvious that the church didn't have a clear picture of where it was headed. Because various leaders and ministries were pulling in different directions, the church wasn't going much of anywhere.

A couple of months ago Ralph, chair of the elder board, said, "Our problem is that we don't have a clear vision." Everyone in the room agreed. So the pastor and elders decided to go away for a weekend and come back with a vision statement. It was a wonderful weekend, and before they headed home they had adopted a twelve-point vision statement.

Over the next four weeks, Pastor Jerry preached on the vision statement, covering three points in each sermon. The elders heard several positive comments about the sermons. They were on their way!

One year later: the elders were discussing a ministry program that required so many volunteers that other ministries were coming up short on workers. Carol commented, "I'm not even sure this ministry is helping us get where we want to go." Jamie chimed in, "I see that not just with this program, but two or three others as well. It seems like our ministry leaders are pulling in a half-dozen different directions."

> **Vision is a picture of God's preferred future for a particular church family.**

The room fell silent. Finally Ralph asked, "Isn't this the same issue we were discussing a year ago? Isn't this why we spent a weekend in the mountains writing out our vision? Is it just me, or does it seem to the rest of you like we're no closer to being on the same page than we were a year ago?"

Almost every church has a mission statement. The church's mission is nonnegotiable. It was given to us by Jesus two thousand years ago. While different churches word it differently, we all have the same mission.

Vision, however, is unique to each church. Vision is a picture of God's preferred future for a particular church family. Vision answers the questions: "What has God uniquely called our church to do and be? If we are fulfilling that vision, what will our church look like three, five, or ten years from now?"

In addition to their mission statements, many churches also have vision statements. For many churches, maybe even most, their vision statements do no more good than they did for the fictional Crossroads church. In fact, a vision statement that isn't working can do more harm than good. Why? Because it creates the illusion that the church has a shared vision when it doesn't; it masks the real problem.

Many churches think that because they have a *vision statement*, they have a *shared vision*. The two are vastly different. Like

Crossroads, most churches with vision statements actually don't have a shared vision, yet some churches that have never drafted a vision statement do have a shared vision.

What every church needs to unify and align all its ministries is a *deeply shared vision*. In fact, creating synergy among all the church's ministries through a deeply shared vision is the starting point for maximizing ministry with limited resources. Without a shared vision, no matter how many *efficiencies* you adopt, your *effectiveness* will be anemic.

What is a *deeply shared vision*? It is a picture of a way to do church and a preferred future for the church that is deeply shared by a critical mass of the church's core leaders. It serves as the lens through which leaders make all major ministry decisions.

Here's how this worked in one church. Through a thrift store ministry, an urban church not only met needs for clothing, but also built relationships with people who came to faith and became part of the church family. After twenty years, though, staffing the store had become a constant struggle and the ministry was no longer bearing fruit as it had earlier. This raised the question: Is this a ministry we should continue? By this time, the church's core leaders had developed a deeply shared vision of where God was taking their church—a vision that had taken a new direction over the past couple of years. The pastor asked, "Is the thrift store part of the picture of where God is taking us, or just part of where we have been?" At once the leaders knew: God had used it in the past, but it was not part of where God was taking them in the future. The decision to close the store was easy.

Before you can have a shared vision, you must first have shared values.

Though the leaders of this church had a shared vision that made this decision easy, they didn't have a vision statement at the time.

What do you do if, like so many other churches, you have a vision statement that is collecting dust? Rather than dusting it off and trying to sell it, it's healthier to throw it out and start over, engaging all your core leaders in developing a deeply shared vision. How, then, do you do that?

Values Come before Vision

A church's vision grows out of its core values. Before you can have a shared vision, you must first have shared values. Church growth expert Aubrey Malphurs explains the relationship between vision and values like this: "A vision answers the question, *What* are we going to do? It gives the ministry its direction. . . . Core values answer the question, *Why* do we do what we do? They supply the reasons behind our vision."[1]

Examples of values some churches have included:

- Lost people matter to God and therefore must matter to us.
- Discipleship takes place best in small groups.
- God has called us to be a church that primarily serves people who are living in or are coming out of a culture of poverty.
- We believe most ministry should be done by teams.
- We are committed to being a church that is great at relationships.
- To encourage creativity, we will reward people for taking ministry risks, within clearly defined boundaries, and will celebrate failures as well as successes.

Four Kinds of Values

In his book *The Advantage*, Patrick Lencioni describes four kinds of values:

- *Core values* are the few—two or three—essential behaviors that define what makes this church different from almost every other church. They are essential to the church's identity and do not change.

- *Permission-to-play values* are minimum values that are expected of any leader in the church.
- *Accidental values* have grown up unintentionally over the years and may not be helpful to the mission of the church.
- *Aspirational values* are characteristics that do not yet characterize the church but that the church needs to develop to be all God wants it to be.[2]

Many churches' value statements include such character qualities as grace, integrity, and faithfulness, or activities such as prayer, corporate worship, evangelism, studying Scripture, equipping the saints for ministry, and small group life. Into which of the four above categories would these "generic" values fall? It depends.

For example, evangelism could be a *permission-to-play value*. The leaders of the church all share a commitment to the Great Commission, and the church is seeing people come to Christ. At the same time, there is nothing about the evangelistic activities of the church that set it apart from most of the other churches in the area.

Or evangelism could be an *aspirational value*—something that the leaders realize the church must become effective at to fulfill their mission, but they realize they have a long way to go.

Or it could be a *core value*. Riverside Church's average attendance has more than doubled over the past nine years, with two-thirds of that growth coming through evangelism. This is not accidental. "Lost people matter to God" is a core belief of Riverside's denomination and the driver for "Experience Grace," the first of three core values that shapes every ministry decision the church makes.[3]

When Values Conflict

Though they might not put them in writing, some churches have actual values that look something like this:

- We care more about protecting our building from wear and tear than we do about ministering to the children of our neighborhood.

- We care more about keeping a style of music we are more comfortable with than we do about communicating the gospel in a way that connects with the people of our community who do not yet know Christ.

- We want our pastor to spend all of his or her time taking care of us, not spending time with unchurched people.

These contrasts highlight values in tension. In most cases, the tension is between *accidental values* and stated values. Taking care of the church facility and ministry to neighborhood children are both positive values. Pastoral care and evangelism are both important. When these values are in tension, leaders are responsible for pointing out the tension and asking people to clarify: Which is more important to us? What do we need to give up to gain something of greater value? How a church prioritizes and balances these values determines what kind of church it is and how effectively it fulfills its mission.

Who Defines the Church's Values?

The church's governing board, led by the pastor, should lead the process of defining the church's values and it should include everyone doing ministry.

Writing down values that are already shaping the church's life can be done fairly quickly. When people hold conflicting values, however, the process of thinking and talking through which values will guide ministry decisions can and should take longer. Defining shared values is a process of opening our minds and hearts to new perspectives and passions and together seeking God's mind.[4]

As you begin to clarify values, you may discover areas where your leaders are not all on the same page. Without shared values, you cannot rally around a shared vision. Yet developing a shared vision cannot be accomplished simply by adopting a vision statement. It requires engaging hearts and minds by listening to one another and seeking God together. One of the most important functions of church leadership is to cultivate a holy discontent with the status quo and a passion to become what God is calling the church to be, a passion shaped by a deeply shared vision.

9

To Make Big Changes, Start with Baby Steps

Eddy: Every church goes through major changes. Most churches eventually make changes that blow up on them.

When Pastor Brian came to Sand Creek Chapel, the rural congregation was aging. Unless something changed, within a decade the church would be in hospice mode. Brian's vision was to lead the church to become more missional and organic, centered in home-based life groups. Brian envisioned multiple campuses throughout the rural region served by the church, with the goal of growing the church to more than a thousand in attendance.

Within a few years, two new campuses had been launched, and a good number of life groups were up and running. Brian even conducted a workshop at a national conference on leading a church through change.

Then the wheels started coming off the wagon. Tensions between Brian and the "old guard" erupted into open conflict. Over eighteen months or so, about a third of the congregation left. Many who remained were hurt and discouraged and no longer invited their friends to church.

Broadway Baptist, on the other hand, was a traditional Southern Baptist church when along came a team of young seminarians who led the congregation through a similar culture shift, making small groups—rather than the Sunday service—the heart of congregational life. When I visited Broadway, it was clear that their new way of doing church was thriving. I asked one of the pastors, "How do your older adults who are not part of the small groups feel about all the changes?"

I loved his answer. "Recently one of our old saints said to me, 'I really don't understand all the changes our church is making, but I do know that I feel more loved than ever, so I'm fine with the changes.'"

> A church's success in navigating major change without crashing comes down to how well they live out one core principle: *change values before you change structures.*

Two churches trying to navigate similar paradigm shifts. One crashed and burned; the other thrived. What made the difference?

Ultimately a church's success in navigating major change without crashing comes down to how well they live out one core principle: *change values before you change structures.*

Why Values Have to Change First

If a traditional church launches a new worship service with a different style of music to reach people who are not attending church, but the congregation has little passion for reaching more people, the new service will fail. People will gripe about the music, about not having everyone in the same worship service, about the pastor dividing his or her attention, about the schedule, and more. Why? Because they value tradition more than they value reaching new people.

On the other hand, if the pastor can ignite a passion for reaching lost people, the people themselves will generate creative ideas for doing this. Those ideas may or may not include launching a new service, but people will be willing to be inconvenienced, to set aside personal preferences, to step outside their comfort zones for the sake of something they value.

The secret to navigating change without crashing is to change values (actual values, not simply stated values) before the church changes its structures. If you skip this step, brace for a crash landing.

Leading Change

When we talk about changing a church's values, obviously we're not talking about eternal values. We're talking about helping people place greater value on those things God values and less value on personal preference and comfort. We're talking about replacing culturally bound traditions with a timeless, biblical vision of what God has called the church to be.

The key player in navigating major change is the senior pastor. That may seem obvious, but we have worked with churches where other staff and leaders were trying to navigate major change without the senior pastor's full support. It doesn't work.

Still, the senior pastor can't do it alone. Change by executive order (unless the change is minor) is the ultimate example of changing structures without first changing values. That's where crashes come from.

The senior pastor doesn't need to have all the skills required to navigate the change. In fact, most senior pastors don't. It takes a team. Navigating major change requires one or more leaders with godly wisdom, strong strategic skills, and a deep understanding of the church's organizational culture. These leaders may be on the church staff, within the congregation, or outside coaches. But the senior pastor must still be the vision caster, leading the charge.

How to Change Values

1. Model the new values.

Pastors who exhort others to evangelize but are not intentionally building relationships with people who are far from God lack credibility. If you as the leader want your congregation to take action based on a passion for reaching out, they need to be hearing stories of how you are building relationships with non-Christian friends.

Pastors who encourage others to join a small group need to be telling stories from their own small groups—how group members serve one another and care for each other in tough times. They need to be sharing why it is important for them to be in a group where they can safely confess their own sins and know they will be encouraged to follow through on the next steps of obedience God is asking them to take.

2. Build strong team relationships with core leaders.

"Change values before you change structures" does not mean that 100 percent of the congregation has to buy into a new value before you introduce change. It means that *a critical mass of your core leaders* must embrace the new value. How does this happen?

> **While leaders need to spend time on management decisions, they need to spend even more time sharing joys and sorrows, sharing deep personal needs, and praying for one another.**

Pastors must invest deeply in relationships with the church's core leaders (formal, informal, and emerging). While leaders need to spend time on management decisions, they need to spend even more time sharing joys and sorrows, sharing deep personal needs, and praying for one another. They need to become an intimate community, a working laboratory where heart change is constantly taking place.

Why? First, because heart change is what God is up to in our lives, but also because heart change equals values change. Through heart-to-heart sharing over time, your leaders can come to deeply share a set of core values. These shared values provide the soil from which shared vision grows.

3. Start small.

Eddy: When Hilltop Urban Church began our transition to becoming a church of house churches, we didn't launch multiple house churches; we started with one. That pilot house church met for eight months to figure out the DNA that fit the culture we were serving and to train the shepherds who would lead house churches. Only when we were confident the DNA was healthy enough to reproduce did we launch multiple house churches. We didn't wait to get it perfect; otherwise we would have been paralyzed. But we did have about 80 percent of the DNA working well and were confident we could continue developing the rest in the new house churches.

When we began our transition from boards and committees to ministry teams, we began with one team. Over the next four years, all of our ministries transitioned to a team approach. Now our leaders would never go back to the old way. Had we tried to transition every ministry at once, it would have blown up and many would have soured on ministry teams.

Why start small? First, so we can learn by trial and error without involving the whole church in our beginner mistakes. Second, so we can start with those who are eager to experiment rather than pushing change on people who don't see a need for it. Third, because most people won't catch a vision of the new way just by reading or hearing about it. They need to see how it works before they can embrace it. When we start with a prototype, skeptics get to see the new way and hear the enthusiasm of those doing it, and that enthusiasm is contagious.

> **When we start with a prototype, skeptics get to see the new way and hear the enthusiasm of those doing it, and that enthusiasm is contagious.**

4. Share stories that showcase the new values.

To encourage the growth of a small group culture, for example, regularly invite people to share during the worship service what

God is doing in their groups. To promote ministry teams, highlight reports of God at work in their teams. Include stories in sermons that model the new values. (*Caution*: Preaching alone cannot drive culture change, but sermons that grow out of what God is doing among the core leaders can invite others to join in.)

5. Don't get too far ahead of your people.

You've probably heard the saying, "If you're ahead of your people but they're not following you, you're not leading; you're just taking a walk."

We are sometimes tempted to see those who are slow to embrace change as obstacles. Yes, there are a few who will never embrace change, but they are a small minority. When you see good people holding back, people who you know love God and the church, don't treat them as adversaries. Talk with them.

About a year into Hilltop's "extreme church makeover," a church survey suggested that trust between the pastor and some members was strained. This surprised the staff. When we took the results to the team responsible to review the survey, they said, "It's obvious: some of our old guard don't understand the changes."

At their request, the pastor and I met with those who had concerns. We affirmed how much we valued them and answered their questions. We were blown away by their enthusiasm about what God was doing, even though some of the changes were outside of their comfort zone. Trust was restored.

6. Let frustration build before changing formal structures.

As people's values change, the old structures get in the way of living out their new values. When people start saying, "We need to change our bylaws; they no longer fit the way we are doing ministry now," it's time to change the bylaws. But if you try to change bylaws because the pastor has a vision for a different way of doing ministry that few understand, bylaw changes won't help.

They may even be divisive. Rather than pushing for basic structural change, hold back until most of your leaders are asking for the change. Then the change process will likely be smooth sailing.

7. Signal your turns.

> **Avoid surprises. Confronted with a big change they haven't had time to process, most people will feel afraid.**

Before rolling out a change that affects much of the congregation—a new service, a new staff position, a change in worship format—take great pains to avoid surprises. Confronted with a big change they haven't had time to process, most people will feel afraid.

Turn signals prevent wrecks. Before you make a big turn, start signaling well ahead of time. Explain. Take questions. Explain some more. Create safe places for people to process. Adopt a "no surprises" rule. If you're almost fanatical about signaling turns, your people will tend to trust you in those rare emergencies when sudden turns can't be avoided.

8. Help people grieve.

> **Once you have a culture of innovation, changes that would previously have taken months or years can be implemented in weeks because people have become accustomed to continual improvements.**

No matter how healthy change is, all change involves loss. These losses are real. Be clear about the tradeoffs: what you gain, what you have to give up. Acknowledge the price that people are paying. Never shame people—"Don't you care about lost people?"—because they find loss painful.

For those of us eager for change, taking the time to change values before changing structures may seem slow. Yes, it does take longer to lay the groundwork. But in addition to avoiding disaster, once the groundwork is laid, the pace of change accelerates. As your people internalize new values, the innovations that grow out of them will far surpass anything the staff alone could have dreamed up. Rather than introducing a single innovation, you will have created a culture of innovation.

Once you have a culture of innovation, changes that would previously have taken months or years can be implemented in weeks because people have become accustomed to continual improvements. When people learn to trust their leaders to navigate change well, transitioning to better ways of doing ministry generates far more excitement than resistance.

Ministry doesn't get much more fun than that.

Part 2

More-with-Less Staffing

10

Hire Equippers
to Multiply Leaders

He gave the apostles, the prophets, the evangelists, the shepherds and teachers, to equip the saints for the work of ministry, for building up the body of Christ.

Ephesians 4:11–12

In this passage Paul highlights two principles foundational to a biblical approach to church staffing. First, every believer is called to do the work of ministry; ministry is not for the special few. Second, God calls some to a specialized role—equipping others for ministry. What does this mean for how we staff the church?

1. We should not hire pastors and teachers primarily to "take care of us" or "do ministry on our behalf." Rather, we are to hire pastors and teachers to equip the rest of us to do ministry.
2. The church needs to free up those God has called to be "equippers of ministers" to devote themselves to their calling rather than expecting them to be "ministers for hire," doing the ministry themselves. An example is when the seven were chosen

in Acts 6 to free up the apostles for "prayer and the ministry of the word" (v. 4 NIV).

Of course, not all equippers are paid staff. Many people in your church are called to equip others. When we hire pastors or ministry directors, though, we need to be clear about what God has and has not called them to do. This is the starting point for a biblical and effective approach to church staffing.

From "Minister for Hire" to "Equipper of Ministers"

What does it look like when a church shifts from hiring people to do ministry to hiring people to equip others to do ministry?

- A church that is following this principle will not hire a student ministries director to pastor all their students. Rather, the church will hire someone to equip those who are called to disciple students. While your student ministries director must relate well to students, it is even more critical that he or she be gifted at developing adult leaders and building a leadership team.

- A children's ministries director will also be hired primarily to build and lead a team of adults who are called to disciple children. A church hired one of their best children's workers to direct children's ministries. Though she was great with kids, she had no gifts for coaching adults or building teams. Under her leadership, most of the children's programs shriveled up and died.

- A traditional minister of music may lead the music every Sunday and personally direct a choir. In contrast, when a church hires an equipper as pastor of worship arts, his or her job is to equip the individuals and teams who contribute to the worship experience. Depending on its size, a church may have multiple worship bands, choirs, ensembles, tech teams, a drama team, a service planning team, and a stage design team. The pastor of worship arts may be one of several worship leaders. The real test of this staff member's effectiveness is whether the quality remains just as high when he or she is out of town.

- In equipping churches, the role of the senior pastor is much different than in chaplaincy churches. While senior pastors may do most of the preaching, they are more likely to share it. Rather than being the primary caregivers, the senior pastors will facilitate the development of teams of caregivers—small group leaders, Stephen ministers, and so on. Members will receive far better pastoral care than if they relied on just the paid staff for their pastoral care needs. Most important, the pastors will spend less time leading ministries themselves and more time coaching ministry leaders and emerging leaders.

From Doer to Equipper

Many church members have superhuman expectations of their pastors. Pastors who try to fulfill those expectations live in constant frustration and eventually burn out. When pastors embrace their calling to be equippers, however, it unburdens them. Here is Pastor Dennis Hesselbarth's story.

> Twenty-six years earlier, I had planted Hilltop Urban Church. Like most inner city churches, Hilltop was plagued by a chronic lack of leadership. Poor education, frequent crises, and relational struggles brought great instability. I resigned myself to importing stable leaders from suburban churches to run our programs, and "doing the rest" myself. It was 24/7 ministry: people in crisis knocking on the door, fund-raising, recruiting, preaching, organizing. Yet I also got lots of strokes—praise for my dedication and impact. I fed on that.
>
> Our community was being served, but deep down I knew lives were not being transformed. Our people remained recipients rather than participants; receivers not givers; followers not leaders.
>
> I knew we needed to lift, to develop, to empower. But how?
>
> Change started with me. Conflict erupted. Family members died. Prized positions were taken away. I was fingered for being

controlling. (I was!) In my own loss and brokenness, I joined a recovery group in our own church.

There I was powerfully ministered to by the uneducated, broken poor—the ones who "couldn't lead." The mutual support of this confidential small group with its focus on vulnerability, heart change, and action (not just head knowledge) transformed hearts and spawned leaders before my eyes. The simple twelve-step group format meant anyone could lead. They came, observed, opened up, and, before long, led.

I learned several crucial lessons from that group. I recognized that I hadn't developed leaders among the broken poor because I didn't truly believe they could be transformed and lead. I also faced up to the fact that I did have a control issue. I liked and needed the praise I received when I did things myself. I had to let go and trust others to lead. Finally, I saw that our complex middle-class programs required a style of leadership that didn't fit most of our people. Launching small, simple peer groups could open a path for growing powerful leaders.

> **I no longer defined my success by what I accomplished, but by the successes of others.**

But I didn't know how to implement what I was learning. God exposed me to a network of cell churches and then brought a church consultant versed in transformative small group and team ministry. We launched a pilot cell/house church and replaced a salaried children's director with a ministry team of inexperienced urban folk. Over the next few years, as our house churches multiplied and new ministry teams were launched, we saw more lives changed and leaders developed than in all the preceding twentysome years combined.

My role increasingly shifted from doing to coaching and training. I no longer defined my success by what I accomplished, but by the successes of others. A preaching team replaced me—I preached less than half the time. Pastoral care moved to our house churches and became far more encompassing. Collaborative teams gave direction and made decisions. Ministry, even through the inevitable ups and downs of urban life, became energizing!

This all culminated with God's leading me to announce my resignation. Our middle-class folks feared for the future. But not our urban folks. Rather than find another full-time pastor, they asked for continued coaching and formed a team of "broken urban folks" to lead the church.

Paul writes:

> For consider your calling, brothers: not many of you were wise according to worldly standards, not many were powerful, not many were of noble birth. But God chose what is foolish in the world to shame the wise; God chose what is weak in the world to shame the strong; God chose what is low and despised in the world, even things that are not, to bring to nothing things that are, so that no human being might boast in the presence of God. (1 Cor. 1:26–29)

There is no greater joy than becoming an equipper, partnering with our God as he transforms the weak and unlikely into powerful agents of his kingdom.

As Pastor Dennis was making this transition, so were the rest of the church staff. During this period the part-time children's director and the full-time youth pastor—both doers—resigned. The church chose not to hire replacements. Instead they created a children's ministry team and a youth ministry team to lead those ministries, and they hired a half-time equipper to coach those two teams, a couple of other teams, and some small group leaders. Over four years Hilltop transitioned from having a staff that was paid to do ministry to having a staff that primarily equipped others to do ministry.

Specialists and Generalists

Many growing churches hire new staff to relieve their overworked senior pastors only to find that their pastors' workloads get heavier, not lighter. Here's why.

There are two basic categories of equipping staff, specialists and generalists. A specialist focuses on one function or age group, such as music, youth, children, or senior adults. A generalist works with the whole congregation. Senior pastors, executive pastors, discipleship pastors, and most associate pastors are generalists.

When hiring their second equipping staff member (after the senior pastor), many churches hire a specialist—a student ministries director, a musician, or a children's director. That can sometimes be appropriate—*if* the position is part-time. If, however, the church's second equipping staff position is a specialist, it usually doesn't lighten the pastor's load, but makes it heavier. Why? Because hiring a specialist takes little off the pastor's plate unless the pastor has been personally directing the youth ministry or worship team, but it adds the major responsibility of supervising a staff member.

If the goal is to lighten the pastor's workload, and the church has already hired excellent support staff, the next step is to hire either a generalist or create a position that combines specialist and generalist responsibilities. The staff will function best if, as it grows, you keep an approximate balance between generalists and specialists.

Equippers of Equippers

By the time a church reaches around 350 in average attendance, the staff needs to include a person gifted at strategic planning, team building, and developing not only leaders, but leaders who can develop other leaders. If your senior pastor has these gifts, great! Otherwise you can meet this need by hiring a director of ministry development, an executive director of ministries, an executive pastor, or an associate pastor with specific responsibilities, depending on the church. While such a person is hugely valuable even in small churches, in larger churches the lack of this kind of staff member becomes a serious barrier to growth.[1]

> The telltale sign of equippers is that their greatest joy comes not from hitting home runs, but from watching the people they are coaching hit home runs.

The Heart of an Equipper

The telltale sign of equippers is that their greatest joy comes not from hitting home runs, but from watching the people they are coaching hit home runs. While they may be gifted at running programs, they prefer to give leadership away to others and coach them and cheer them on as they lead. They don't need to be in the limelight because they aren't after significance, recognition, appreciation, or validation. Rather, when they receive praise, they instinctively refocus the spotlight: "Oh, I have a great team; they deserve the credit." This isn't false modesty; it is the heart of a person whose greatest passion is developing other people.

When a church builds an equipping staff made up of such people, it shifts from *adding* leaders to *multiplying* leaders. This timeless principle from Ephesians 4 is the foundation for more-with-less staffing. Bringing together an equipping team, though, is just the first step. Many churches hire equippers only to frustrate them with time demands that pull them away from their calling. The next chapter looks at how to avoid this common pitfall.

——— Pay Your Staff to Pray ———

Are you tired? Worn out? Burned out on religion? Come to me. Get away with me and you'll recover your life. I'll show you how to take a real rest. Walk with me and work with me—watch how I do it. Learn the unforced rhythms of grace. I won't lay anything heavy or ill-fitting on you. Keep company with me and you'll learn to live freely and lightly.

Matthew 11:28–30 Message

The way I was doing the work of God was destroying the work of God in me.

Bill Hybels

Many, many pastors often minister out of an emotional tank that is less than half full. As a general rule, pastors are on call 24/7. In Acts 6, the apostles appointed seven helpers (support staff) so they could devote themselves to the priorities God had called them to—"prayer and the ministry of the word" (v. 4 NIV). One of the greatest needs of any church is for its pastors to regularly spend uninterrupted blocks of time with God. If your pastors aren't hearing from God, the whole church is in trouble. If your pastors are running on empty, they can't minister to you out of the overflow.

We recommend that you make it the number-one requirement in the job descriptions of all your equipping staff to regularly take extended times of solitude to hear from God and for spiritual renewal. This is not a day off to spend with family or to take care of things at home. We suggest that pastors and other full-time equipping staff spend a half day every week or a full day every other week practicing personal renewal in this way. For burned-out staff members, a full day a week is needed until they are restored.

These times of spiritual retreat may include reading Scripture and other spiritual literature, journaling, listening to or singing worship music, prayer walking, meeting with a spiritual director or spiritual friend (discipleship partner), spending time in nature, or even taking a nap.

This retreat time should normally be taken not at the office or at home, but at a place where the staff member will be contacted only in an emergency such as a retreat center, a cabin, a lake, or a library. Have a reporting process to hold your equipping staff accountable for using this time as intended.

When one pastor started taking regular spiritual retreat days, he was surprised to find that he got scolded whenever he missed them. Why? Because members could tell the difference in his sermons. It wasn't because he was using that time to prepare sermons; it was because he was hearing from God during his retreat time, and if he wasn't hearing from God, the people could tell.

11

The Case of the
Overpaid Secretary

Thousands of churches pay way too much for secretarial work. Why? Because they hire professionals with seminary degrees, pay them a professional salary, and then expect them to spend much of their time doing secretarial work for which they are not trained.

If you had asked the members of New Creation Fellowship if they had a full-time pastor, they would have said yes. But they would have been wrong. While New Creation was paying for a full-time pastor, they weren't getting one. Why not? Since New Creation had no other staff, Pastor Steve was actually a two-thirds-time pastor, a one-fourth-time secretary, and a one-twelfth-time custodian. Because this had been going on for years, not surprisingly, the church's average attendance had never reached one hundred.

One of the biggest ways churches waste staffing dollars is by skimping on support staff. If a pastor being paid $60,000 a year spends ten to fifteen hours a week doing things that an office assistant could do better, the church is paying the pastor about $15,000 for work that a part-time assistant could do more efficiently for a fraction of that cost. More important, the pastor is not spending that time equipping. For many pastors, detailed office work not only steals their time but also drains them emotionally, decreasing their effectiveness as spiritual leaders. More-with-less staffing happens when equippers are freed up by doers—support staff—so they can spend most of their time equipping.

> **More-with-less staffing happens when equippers are freed up by doers—support staff—so they can spend most of their time equipping.**

Support staff includes office staff, facility staff, and, in larger churches, ministry assistants.

Office Staffing

Is there a right ratio between equipping staff and office support staff? What gifts and competencies does a church office staff need? Is it better to hire members or outsiders to staff a church office?

These aren't the kind of high-drama questions likely to inspire a blockbuster movie, but getting your office team right makes a world of difference in the effectiveness of your staff team and the church as a whole.

1. What is a good staffing ratio?

A good rule of thumb is to hire one full-time office employee for every two equipping staff members. In addition, your senior pastor often needs full-time office support to reach full productivity. This doesn't mean that every small church needs a full-time secretary. It does mean that by the time the church's attendance reaches 150, it should have about forty hours of office support. Office support staff includes secretaries, receptionists, administrative assistants, bookkeepers, office managers, and those who oversee social media and communications.

Equipping staff (Full-time equivalent)	Office support staff (Full-time equivalent)	Attendance capacity
1	1.0	150
2	1.5	300
3	2.0	450
4	2.5	600
5	3.0	750
10	5.5	1500

Many healthy churches have a higher or lower staffing ratio depending on their staffing philosophy. There is more than one right answer, but this is a good starting point for estimating your needs.

2. What spiritual gifts are best for office staff?

Of the seven motivational gifts listed in Romans 12:6–8, three are essential for office staff.

- *Compassion* is the most important gift for receptionists. A person with the gift of compassion will consistently make a person calling or visiting the office feel like he or she is the most important person in the world. If you have a person with the gift of compassion at your reception desk, people will want to sit and talk with your receptionist, especially if they are going through a tough time. While there must be reasonable limits on this, affirm this ministry of listening as a core part of your receptionist's role.
- *Serving* is the gift most needed for routine secretarial duties. A person with this gift finds joy in doing repetitive tasks with excellence week after week. Servers are often good at creating office systems and organizing data.
- *Administration* is the critical spiritual gift for office managers. While servers are usually great at organizing things and data, administrators are gifted at organizing people and teams and getting results through others.

It is rare for someone to score high on all three of these gifts on a spiritual gift survey, but it is common to score high on two.[1] For a church with a single secretary, the compassion-serving gift combination is ideal. When the second office staff member is added, one should be the office manager, overseeing the other. A mistake many churches make at this point is promoting the secretary/receptionist to office manager based on seniority. Unless the secretary has the gift of administration, he or she will flounder in the new role, and the church may lose a gifted receptionist.

One other motivational gift can be a real plus in the office—the gift of *giving*. While we tend to associate this gift with money, people who score high on this gift are passionate about championing the ministries of the leaders they support. People who have this gift along with serving or administration can make great administrative assistants.

3. Should we hire insiders or outsiders?

The pros and cons of hiring church members to work in the office are fairly obvious.

PROS

- Attenders already know the other attenders.
- Attenders already know the culture of the church. They get up to speed faster.
- Most insiders who join an office staff are motivated by love for their church.

CONS

- There may not be any available church attenders with the needed skills.
- Office workers may find it hard to worship because people keep asking for office assistance before, during, and after worship services.
- It is harder to terminate church insiders than outsiders. Terminating someone who is part of the church can trigger church conflict.

- The church may be more tempted to keep attenders on payroll to provide for their financial needs even when their work is unsatisfactory.

- Some church insiders may gossip or violate confidentiality. Those outside the church's social network are less likely to do this.

So, is it better to hire insiders or outsiders? As a general rule, the more office workers interact with members and ministry volunteers, the more important it is for them to be hired from within. It is a huge advantage for the receptionist to be an insider. Because of frequent contact with volunteers, the same is true for administrative assistants working with children, students, and small groups.

On the other hand, bookkeepers, financial secretaries, graphic designers, and webmasters can all be hired from outside. These roles can also be contracted out to other agencies or home-based freelancers.

What about all those potential cons of hiring from within? The key is to hire with your eyes wide open, taking pains to avoid all these potholes.

- Hire attenders only if they are truly qualified for the job. If no attender is qualified, hire from outside.

- Communicate to the congregation that the office staff is not on duty when they come to worship. If you need office coverage during services, staff the office with volunteers or hire someone for those hours.

- When you hire, set the bar high for office skills and even higher for people skills so terminations are rare.

- The church needs to hire capable staff, and it also needs to help attenders in financial need. Keep these responsibilities separate. *Do not* hire based on financial need.

- *Never* hire gossips or people with a divisive or critical spirit, no matter how impressive their skills! Few church cancers are more deadly than an employee who "stirs the pot."

4. How can we empower unpaid equipping staff?

If, as the previous chapter suggests, unpaid ministry leaders are included in your staff, one of the most important ways you can empower them is by giving them full office support. While this might at first seem like an added expense, it can actually be a powerful more-with-less staffing strategy.

When the youth pastor at a church of about three hundred moved on, the pastor debated whether to hire a part-time replacement or to rely on volunteers to lead the ministry. We suggested the church hire a half-time administrative assistant who would support the volunteer youth ministry team and children's ministry team ten hours a week each. When a church has strong volunteer teams, it is sometimes far more cost-effective to hire support staff rather than part-time equipping staff for these ministries. This frees the ministry teams to put most of their time into working with the children and students without having to put long hours into office work each week.

Facility Staffing

Many pastors and other equipping staff spend several hours a month doing facility work—setting up and tearing down rooms; coordinating with repair professionals, exterminators, and inspectors; and arriving early to unlock the building and staying late to lock up. A key part of the facility staff's mission, like that of the office staff, is to protect the equipping staff from being distracted from what they are called to do.

Facility staff includes custodians, maintenance staff, groundskeepers, and, in larger churches, facility managers. Medium and large churches hire administrators or business managers whose job includes oversight of facilities and facility staff. A few tips:

- If you have a multiple-use facility, as described in the next section of this book, hire staff to set up and tear down multiple-use rooms. This protects not only your equipping staff, but also your volunteer leaders. If worship leaders and teachers have to set up and tear down for their activities, it will wear them out and soon sour them on multiuse space. If you have a lot of set up and tear down on Sunday morning, consider hiring a few hours of help. Hiring people to set up and tear down is a key to making multiple-use facilities work long-term.

- A building that looks unloved turns people away. Once volunteers can no longer stay on top of repairs, hire a maintenance person. Some churches need to do this before attendance reaches one hundred; others can wait till they hit three or four hundred. It depends on your facility and your building and grounds team.

- Streamline routine decisions. Empower facility staff to make routine budgeted repairs without running them by the trustees. When you hire an administrator or business manager who oversees facilities, shift maintenance decisions from trustees to staff.

Ministry Assistants

Many medium and large churches have a third category of support staff—ministry assistants. Ministry assistants are typically a hybrid of administrative assistants and program directors. They often provide office assistance for an equipping staff member and also direct a program. A children's ministry assistant, for example, might coordinate children's church or a weeknight children's ministry, or oversee one session of Sunday school, in addition to providing office support. Ministry assistants also commonly work in student ministries, worship arts, and connections ministry. Ministry assistants are paid more than office support staff but less than equipping staff. When a growing ministry needs more staff, hiring a ministry assistant rather than another equipping staff member is sometimes an effective more-with-less strategy.

More Than Hiring the Right People

To build a more-with-less staff, your pastors and ministry leaders, paid and unpaid, need to be equippers, not just doers. They need to be teamed up with support staff who free your equippers to invest most of their time and energy equipping others rather than doing. But filling your staff with capable equippers and doers isn't enough. A more-with-less staff has that something extra that makes the whole more than the sum of its parts. That is the focus of our next chapter.

12

Build a Dream Team

If you are a sports fan, you have sometimes watched star-studded teams struggle to win while less talented teams win consistently. What makes the difference? Teamwork. With great teamwork, the whole is greater than the sum of the parts.

Many churches cobble together a staff one person at a time with little thought to forging a team. Approaching staffing as strategic team-building rather than slot-filling is at the heart of more-with-less staffing. *Staff team*, as used here, does not equal *employees*. It rarely includes all the church's employees and may include unpaid staff members. Who makes up the staff team depends on roles, not employment. The staff team is the team responsible *for planning and leading the implementation of the church's vision.*

The Ministry of Leading Staff

Every pastor we know believes shepherding is important. Some are better at pastoral care than others; some enjoy it and some don't. But all agree it is essential. Every pastor we know believes preaching is important. Some are better at it than others. Some enjoy it more than others. But all agree it is essential.

When it comes to leading staff, though, we've found something surprising. It doesn't surprise us that some pastors are better at it than others. It doesn't surprise us that some enjoy it more than others. What surprises us is how many pastors don't think it's important, and how many treat it as a minor chore that can be squeezed into the cracks between "real" ministry responsibilities. Some act like shepherding and preaching are spiritual, but leading the staff team is somehow unspiritual or unimportant.

> **Some pastors act like shepherding and preaching are spiritual, but leading the staff team is somehow unspiritual or unimportant.**

Whether the staff team is paid or unpaid, a senior pastor has no more important responsibility than to build the strongest possible staff team and lead it well. Along with preaching and shepherding, this is at the heart of the pastor's work. It takes time. It takes discipline. It takes skill. It takes study and hard work. If the pastor is not gifted at building and leading teams, it is critical for the pastor to partner with someone who is. The effectiveness of the staff—and the church's ministry—depend on it.

Six Characteristics of a Dream Team

High-performance ministry teams have six basic characteristics: small *size*, shared *call*, single *focus*, healthy *relationship*, real *empowerment*, and full *collaboration*. In most churches, the staff team in the most important team. When the staff team is hitting on all six cylinders, it serves as an example for all the other teams in the church, greatly increasing the possibility of a healthy team culture throughout the church.

A dysfunctional staff team cripples a church. A dream team multiplies its effectiveness. A dream team is one that is fulfilling its assignment—planning and leading the implementation of the church's vision—while embodying the six characteristics of effective ministry teams.

A ministry team is . . .

A small group of people (Size)
Who are all called (Call)
To the same ministry (Focus)
Who love and trust each other (Relationship)
And who decide, within boundaries, how to (Empowerment)
Do that ministry together (Collaboration)

1. Size: "A small group of people."

The staff team—the group charged with planning and leading the implementation of the church's vision—is small, whatever the church's size. When Living Stones team member Ken Dean was executive pastor of Fellowship Bible Church in Little Rock, Arkansas, weekly attendance averaged 6500. When he met with his paid staff each Monday, there were 120 people in the room. That was not, though, where the work of what we are calling the staff team took place. That was done by an executive team of six or seven.

Hilltop Urban Church averages about sixty in attendance. Their staff team is made up of six team leaders, two paid and four unpaid. Though one church is huge and the other small, their staff teams are about the same size. Why? Because great team dynamics require a small group—three to twelve, with five to eight the ideal number.

Hilltop's unpaid staff are as fully staff team members as the paid staff. They are listed on the church bulletin, provided office space (though some prefer to work from home), and given secretarial support. Most importantly, these six staffers together evaluate, plan, and lead the church in implementing the church's vision.

2. Call: "Who are called."

How do you get the right people on the team—people passionate about and gifted for their ministries, who bring out the best in each other?

As the staff team leader, the senior pastor has the primary responsibility for building the staff. When a board or committee has the formal authority to hire staff, if they are wise they will ask the senior pastor to take the lead in hiring and will assist by giving their advice and consent. If they discover something that disqualifies a candidate, they should, of course, withhold consent. Absolutely never, however, should a search committee hire a staff member, paid or unpaid, without the senior pastor's full support. Only when a team leader is responsible for the makeup of the team can that leader be held responsible for the team's results.

For some excellent pastors, however, this is not an area of strength. A pastor of a church of six hundred was an incredible Bible teacher but struggled with staffing. Half of his key staff members had job descriptions that didn't match their gifts. So he hired a former business executive to oversee staff. On paper this looked like a great hire, but the new staff member, rather than bringing order, created even more chaos. Because this pastor didn't understand the skills needed for the new position and wasn't able to detect whether a person had the needed skills, he made a disastrous hire.

How can pastors who are not strong in this area build a dream team? By involving others who have these gifts. Most pastors are good judges of character. Most are good judges of whether a candidate is aligned with their vision and philosophy of ministry. Fewer, though, are gifted in creating and streamlining systems and navigating organizational change. When this is the case, pastors are wise to seek the counsel of church members who have a track record of building teams that get great results, whether in the church, business, or volunteer work. If no church members have these skills, outside coaching can help the church build its dream team and avoid painful mistakes. While the pastor makes the final call on key hires, when others have expertise in building a staff team the wise pastor will draw on their wisdom.

3. Focus: "To the same ministry."

The six characteristics of ministry teams apply to every ministry team. What sets the staff team apart is its specific assignment: *planning and leading the implementation of the church's vision.*

In considering whether someone should join your staff team, it is not enough to ask, "Would this person direct this area of ministry well?" You must also ask, "Is this person passionate about our vision, our shared picture of God's preferred future for our church? Is he or she fully committed to our values—the principles that guide how we do ministry?"

If staff members don't share the church's vision and values, if they cannot or will not play from the shared score, they need to leave the staff. One associate pastor announced, "I believe this church's vision is admirable, but I don't think it's realistic." Because he didn't believe the vision could be achieved, he wasn't even trying to achieve it. He soon resigned, as he should have. A team member who does not believe in the vision cannot help the team win.

4. Relationship: "Who love and trust each other."

In *The Five Dysfunctions of a Team*, author Patrick Lencioni names the first dysfunction as lack of trust.[1] Trust is foundational. Everything else the team does, he says, builds on it. In the churches we work with, most ministry teams are stuck at this level. They haven't developed a deep trust for each other. Until your group gets this right, you don't really have a team. You may have a committee or a working group. You may get some things done. But you don't have a team.

Eddy: Most of the team meetings in my church begin with a shared meal. During the meal we do "happy/sad"—we each share something from the week that we feel happy about and something we feel sad about. This is not idle chitchat; it is relationship building.

After eating we ask each other, "What do you need Jesus to do for you today?" then pray for each other. We are getting to know each other at the heart level. We are learning to care about each other as people, not just as coworkers. We are growing trust.

The leader must take the lead in developing trust by *being vulnerable*. When I am vulnerable in a group, I make it safe for others to be vulnerable. Most of our church's team leaders are amazingly vulnerable. They share their struggles. They admit their mistakes. They aren't afraid to say, "I'm not good at that; I need your help."

One pastor responded to this idea by saying, "I don't do vulnerability." He was right. He responded defensively to feedback, blamed others, and seldom admitted he was wrong. How did this impact the staff? Trust was near zero. Staff members dreaded coming to work. Bad behaviors in the staff and congregation were swept under the rug. People were leaving the congregation in droves.

> **A healthy staff team models teamwork for every other team in the church.**

If you "don't do" vulnerability, either get the help you need to learn to be appropriately vulnerable or else don't inflict yourself on a team as its leader. Discretion is essential, of course. Don't use team meetings as therapy sessions. Don't confess other people's sins in the name of "just being honest." Do own up to it when you behave badly or drop the ball. Admit when you don't know the answer or when you're not good at something. A leader who refuses to be vulnerable dooms the group to being something less than a team.

A healthy staff team models teamwork for every other team in the church. You will rarely find a church where most of the ministry teams are thriving unless the staff team is showing the way.

5. Empowerment: "And who decide, within boundaries, how to."

The principle of empowerment—those who are called to the ministry decide how to do it—is the dynamo of teamwork. How often do we give people jobs to do then tie their hands?

- A church hired an office manager, but then did not give her authority to upgrade software or buy office equipment, though it was in the budget.

- A church hired a facility manager, but required him to wait on trustee approval for any repair over a hundred dollars.
- An elder scolded an associate pastor about how he was doing his job, but the elder's expectations conflicted with the senior pastor's. The associate pastor wasn't sure whose direction he was expected to follow.
- A church board required its pastors to be in the office from nine to five, five days a week, keeping them from spending time in the community.
- The leaders of a children's ministry couldn't change their program's name until the congregation voted on it.

When we give people responsibility without authority, we set them up for frustration and failure. In *Winning on Purpose*, author John Edmund Kaiser describes the four key roles in the church:

- The congregation ministers.
- The pastor leads.
- The board governs.
- The staff manages.[2]

Most church boards spend most of their time bogged down in managing rather than governing. While small churches can get by with this, it becomes burdensome in the medium church and paralyzing for the large church.[3] The more a board gets out of the management business and empowers the staff to do its job—implement the church's vision—the more effective the staff will be, assuming your staff is made up of good managers. (If your staff members aren't good managers, you have made some staffing mistakes.) Almost all operating decisions can be made faster and better by those actually leading the ministries.

> **The more a board gets out of the management business and empowers the staff to do its job—implement the church's vision—the more effective the staff will be.**

This doesn't mean the staff can do whatever they please. The staff team, like every other team, makes decisions *within boundaries*. Defining those boundaries is the board's responsibility.

6. Collaboration: "Do that ministry together."

When the staff meets they are members of the staff team first—with responsibility for the overall ministry of the church—and team leaders second. They take off their specialist hats (children, students, worship) and put on their generalist hats (moving the whole church forward toward its vision). The staff members' highest loyalty must be not to the teams they lead, but to the team they are members of—the staff team.

The staff team evaluates ministry. They dream and plan for activities that cross department boundaries and break down silos. The worship arts leader can speak into children's ministry and the business manager can help brainstorm student ministry.

Together the staff team sets budget priorities. Rather than each one lobbying for his or her department, all ask, "How can we fully fund our highest priorities so we can fulfill God's vision for our church?" If the top priority this year is strengthening small groups, the student ministries pastor may offer to give up a trip so small group leaders can go to a training event.

The whole team wins or loses together because they all have the same goal.

Who Leads Staff Meetings?

In some churches one person—the senior pastor or executive pastor, for example—leads the staff meeting. In other cases, different people might lead various parts of the meeting. One gives a devotional, another leads a sharing and prayer time, one handles calendar coordination, while another leads the ministry evaluation and planning.

Few pastors have the gifts to handle all these roles alone. God gave each of us certain gifts and withheld other gifts from us so that *we would have to do ministry together.* Effective team leaders invite others with complementary gifts to share leadership. A pastor who does this well can build a powerhouse staff team.

When your staff team is made up of people with complementary gifts, when it spends more time equipping others to do ministry than doing ministry, when it exhibits the six characteristics of effective ministry teams—you've got your dream team.

Part 3

More-with-Less Buildings

13

Confessions of a Surprised Architect

Ray: A suburban Philadelphia congregation was bursting at the seams. To make room for continuing growth, they proposed building a thousand-seat sanctuary, classrooms, offices, and fellowship space. They asked me to advise them on the design. It seemed obvious: it was time to build.

To determine how best to design their facility, I immersed myself for days in conducting an in-depth study of the church's ministries, finances, staff, day school, building utilization, and site, along with jurisdictional requirements. When I was confident I had a thorough working understanding of the church's facility needs, I met with the board and presented my initial recommendation: "What you really need to build," I announced, "is a storage shed."

Had the church invited me a few years earlier, when I was a practicing architect, my advice would have been far different. "Yes!" I would have told them. "A new sanctuary will draw you and others closer to God. Your community will respond to this beautiful addition. No doubt, there will be financial growth to pay for the project. A bigger, well-designed building will translate into greater ministry."

I had heard all these claims from pastors and church boards, and I had believed them all. But then a surprising change in my life caused me to look at the church through new eyes and forced me to rethink the conventional wisdom that had guided my advice to churches for three decades.

Discovering More-with-Less Church Building

If anyone had suggested I would soon change careers, I would probably have laughed. I had studied to be an architect, spent all my working life as an architect, and after building my own firm and spending twenty-six years as a principal had no intention of ever being anything but an architect.

Then one day as I was driving to our Twin Falls, Idaho, office to meet with one of my partners, a thought came to me as clearly as if someone had entered the car and spoken to me: *There's going to be a big change in your life and it's going to involve your profession.* I recognized the voice. When I got home, I told my wife, Sally, about it, then promptly forgot it.

Three weeks later I had a totally unexpected opportunity to leave my architectural firm when one of my partners, over lunch, offered to buy my stock. I had absolutely no idea what prompted his offer. When I told Sally about it, she said, "No way!" But as we prayed about it, both Sally and I felt we should accept.

"But, Lord," I said, "then I'll have no work and no income. What am I supposed to do?"

God's answer was clear even if a bit sketchy on details: *I'll show you what kind of work you are to do and give you all the work you can handle.* On the strength of that promise I accepted my partner's offer and left behind an established career for an unknown future.

The day after I signed the papers dissolving my association with the firm, Sally and I were on our way to Canada for our first consulting job. A church in Red Deer, Alberta, had asked me to conduct a feasibility study to determine whether they should renovate their existing building or relocate to a larger site. Though it was just my first day wearing my consultant hat, I felt at once the difference it made. Even if the church were to decide to build, I knew I would not be their architect. I don't suppose the possibility of advising a church *not* to build had ever crossed my mind before. But at Red Deer, for the first time, it was a live option.

As an architect, my job had been to follow instructions, to design whatever kind of building the church asked for. When I became a consultant, though, my job changed. I had to advise the church on what was best for the church and that meant looking at the big picture. I analyzed the church's finances. I charted growth patterns. I studied utilization patterns of the existing building. At Red Deer I ended up advising the church to remodel and grow right where they were.

> **I don't suppose the possibility of advising a church *not* to build had ever crossed my mind before.**

But the biggest surprise of that consultation came as I was about to leave. "Ray," the pastor said, "do you know what you are?"

"No," I answered, "I really don't."

"What you are," he said, "is a church growth specialist."

And though that thought was totally new to me, it rang true. God had called me to invest the next chapter of my life in helping churches reach out more effectively.

That didn't mean, though, that I had the expertise my new role demanded, a point soon driven home when another church board peppered me with church-growth questions I couldn't answer. So for the next year I spent much of my time between consultations reading about ministry and church growth, learning from others, and asking the Holy Spirit to teach me. I began to relate what I was learning about church growth to what I already knew about architectural design. I studied church finance and was surprised to learn that the Bible clearly describes financial principles that can guide the work of the church, principles much different from those followed by the world—and by most churches.

By the time the Philadelphia church asked for my help, I realized that a facility plan intended to maximize ministry could not be created in a vacuum. It had to be developed hand in hand with a ministry plan, a staffing plan, and a financial plan. All four had to work together. Because I had looked at the church's facility needs not in isolation but in light of ministry needs and finances, I had come to a conclusion that was startling, at least to me: a major building program at that time would in all likelihood stop the church's growth and create financial bondage for years to come.

Over the next ten years I consulted with scores of churches and learned from each of them. Because I asked facility questions from the new perspective of ministry and outreach, time after time I was forced to admit that some point of conventional wisdom I had embraced as an architect was untrue. Much of this conventional wisdom encouraged churches to build too big, build too soon, or build the wrong kind of building.

> **The single most valuable lesson a church can learn about building is *when not to build*.**

After thirty years of designing and encouraging churches to build new church buildings, it was painful to admit how much of my well-intentioned advice had been misguided. I could see how some churches had actually been hurt by the building programs I had helped with. Some building programs had diverted attention from meeting people's needs. Other churches had taken on building debts that financially crippled their ministries. In many cases the building program had slowed or stopped the growth that had prompted the new building.

These painful lessons eventually pushed me to a conclusion so unconventional that it sounds like architectural heresy: most churches thinking of building *shouldn't*, at least not yet. I became convinced, in fact, that the single most valuable lesson a church can learn about building is *when not to build*. And that lesson can be summarized in three parts—three situations in which a church should not build.

When the Reasons for Building Are Wrong

First, a church should not build if its reasons for building are wrong. Richard Foster describes a congregational meeting his church held to pray for God's guidance concerning a proposed building program.

> I went into the meeting thinking that probably we should build, and left certain that we should not. The crucial turning point came when I saw the driving force behind my desiring that building to be my unarticulated feeling that a building program was the sign of a successful pastor. Theologically and philosophically, I did not believe that, but as we worshiped the Lord, the true condition of my heart was revealed. Eventually, we decided against building, a decision now validated by hindsight.[1]

Years ago a church of about 150 people in Arkansas hired me as an architect to design a new sanctuary for them. When I saw their building, I was puzzled. Though the building was older, its location was good and the congregation had never filled it.

Finally, I asked the pastor, "Why do you want a new building?"

"The first reason," he answered, "is that these people haven't done anything significant for twenty-five years. This is a way to get them to do something significant. Second, the people aren't giving at anywhere near the level they could or should be. A building program would motivate them to give more. Third, a building program will unite the people behind a common goal."

I believed he was right on all three counts and designed the new sanctuary. Now I know that this pastor was trying to do something that never works—solve non-building problems with a building. That church built for the wrong reasons.

When There Is a Better, Less Costly Solution

Second, a church should not build when there is a better way to meet space needs. As I studied the Philadelphia church, I agreed at once that it had a space problem. At its rate of growth, the congregation would soon outgrow its worship space. Between Sunday school and their Christian school, their educational space was full. They had no room for additional staff offices. Building was the obvious solution, and I was tempted to lapse into my traditional architect role to produce the design.

But a thousand-seat sanctuary was the wrong answer. My recommendations startled them. "I found rooms with missionary boxes," I told the board. "Now, those boxes don't need heat. They don't need windows or carpet, do they?" I suggested they build a low-cost storage and maintenance building to empty several rooms currently being used to store missionary boxes, program supplies, seasonal items, and maintenance equipment and supplies.

"This barn on your property is a historic structure," I told them. "It's worth preserving. But you're not getting good use out of it." Then we discussed how they could remodel it into a gymnasium, kitchen, and educational space at half the cost of a comparable new structure.

"You can meet your need for worship space for years to come," I went on, "without the tremendous commitment of time, energy, and money involved in building a new sanctuary." The wall between the existing sanctuary and foyer could be removed to enlarge the worship area. A modest addition could provide them with a new, larger foyer, making it practical to hold two Sunday morning services, which would double their worship seating capacity. The new addition could also house the office space they would soon need for their growing staff.

Finally, I suggested they replace the fixed worship seating with movable seating. For the comparatively low cost of new chairs, the church could use the largest single space in the building for a wide range of activities—space that would otherwise lie useless for all but a few hours a week.

The church accepted the suggestions and completed their remodeling and modest construction projects within a couple of years. The church continued to reach out to the unchurched and within six years grew from 300 to 850.

At this church I first began to realize that of the many churches that had hired me to design new buildings, few actually needed them. Most needed to find ways to use their existing buildings more effectively. While fully using space may sometimes require remodeling, refurnishing, or making modest additions, in many cases it requires no money at all, only a willingness to do things differently. What seems obvious to me now came then as a fresh revelation: until a church is fully using the space it has, it does not need more.

When the Church Risks Financial Bondage

Third, a church should not build when building would increase the risk of financial bondage. A congregation of about 175 in the Seattle area brought me in as a consultant, but only after they had put up the shell of their new building. Someone had offered the church a piece of land visible from the interstate at a bargain price. The church had jumped at it.

Confident that an attractive, highly visible building would make a strong statement to the community about the church's importance and would stimulate growth, they were building a luxurious thousand-seat sanctuary. "We didn't want the inconvenience of building in phases," the pastor explained, "so we decided to build it all at once. I believed that if we just had the faith and the vision, God would provide the money."

By the time I arrived on the scene the church, for all practical purposes, was bankrupt. All I could do was empathize with them and sadly recommend that they board up the unfinished shell, keep on using their old building, and concentrate on growth until future developments enabled them to complete their move.

The Philadelphia church faced a similar risk. When they commissioned my study, they were still in debt for their existing building and planned to borrow most of the money for their new one. This would mean taking out a loan larger than the current congregation could repay on the assumption that future growth would enable them to make the payments.

I prepared a detailed financial analysis projecting the impact such a debt could have on the ministry and growth of the church. After extensive discussions the church leaders concluded such a large debt would risk not only the church's growth but even its existing ministries. They adopted a plan to pay off their current debt and prepare to build future facilities debt-free.

Three Principles for More-with-Less Building

These three situations in which it is a mistake to build—when a church's reason for building is wrong, when there is a better way to meet space needs, and when building would risk financial bondage—suggest three positive principles. These principles can guide churches to decide when it is time to build and what alternatives they have when building is premature.

1. *The Principle of Focus.* A church should build only when it can do so without shifting its focus from ministering to people to building a building.
2. *The Principle of Use.* A church needs more space only when it is fully using the space it already has.
3. *The Principle of Provision.* A church should build only when it can do so within the income God has provided and without using funds needed for the church's present and future ministries to people.

For more than thirty years, these three principles have guided our work with growing churches. Each year we see more evidence of their power to unleash the church to do its real work. They have enabled congregations to leave behind limiting ways of thinking about, using, and paying for church buildings in favor of new ways of thinking that free up most of the time, money, and energy traditionally spent on buildings and invest them in the work of the kingdom.

The Principle of Focus

A church should build only when it can do so without shifting its focus from ministering to people to building a building.

14

Can Building Kill Church Growth?

Ray: After organizing with forty-eight members, Champlain Church grew within four years to an average attendance of 116, filling their rented meeting space to overflowing. To make room for more growth, the church took the next logical step: they built. But then

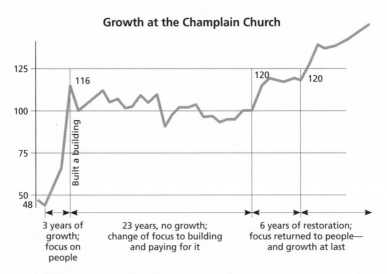

Growth at the Champlain Church

3 years of growth; focus on people

23 years, no growth; change of focus to building and paying for it

6 years of restoration; focus returned to people— and growth at last

a surprising thing happened—the growth suddenly stopped. Over the next twenty-nine years, average attendance fluctuated between 90 and 120. The potential of the new building went unfulfilled.

While conventional wisdom says that church buildings promote growth, the experience of Champlain Church is actually more common: church buildings often kill church growth. In over fifty years as a church architect and consultant, I have seen it happen time and again. An excited, growing congregation builds to make room for continued growth only to see growth stop as soon as they build.

A Shift in Focus

Now, I'm not against church buildings. After all, I am an architect. I have designed buildings for churches most of my life. There is a right time and a right way to build. But in far too many cases building programs have killed or at least slowed the growth of vital congregations. Why?

Champlain Church made nine common mistakes that put the church's growth on hold for three decades.

1. *Believing that building a facility was the work of the church.*
2. *Shifting focus from people to building*—planning, financing, and construction.
3. *Building too soon.* In our economy *at least* 150 to 200 people (average attendance) are normally needed to pay for a major building program without shortchanging staffing and ministry needs. Waiting to build until average attendance reaches three hundred is much less risky, if at all possible.
4. *Building too much.* Champlain's building was too big and too costly for a church its size.
5. *Overlooking staffing needs.* Champlain spent so much on building that they couldn't afford to staff for growth. Adding more seating capacity without first increasing ministry capacity is usually counterproductive.

6. *Failing to consider cost-effective alternatives to building* such as adding a second service, renting a larger space, or starting a satellite congregation.

7. *Failing to budget for unexpected costs during construction.*

8. *Failing to anticipate the costs of operating the new building.*

9. *Assuming the local economy would remain strong.* Every economy has ups and downs, but many churches take on debt without planning for the down times. After Champlain finished its building, the local military base closed, causing the local economy to shrink and members to move away.

Most church growth happens because a church effectively ministers to people's needs. The focus is on people. But often, when a growing church builds, its focus shifts from people to building. That change of focus kills growth.

Losing Focus before Building Begins

A building program can change a church's focus even before construction begins. An established urban congregation of three hundred built a multipurpose building used for worship on Sunday and as a gymnasium and for a host of other events during the week. They thought of this gym as a temporary meeting space to be replaced as soon as possible by a "real sanctuary." Over the next six years, the church grew to seven hundred. At that point the church's leaders spent three years planning and raising funds for a new sanctuary. During those three years, the church's growth slowed to almost zero. Why?

> **Often when a growing church builds, its focus shifts from people to building. That change of focus kills growth.**

Unlike Champlain, debt was not a barrier. The leaders were careful not to commit so much to the building that it would endanger the staffing and funding of ministries. Rather, the church's leaders put so much time and energy into planning the building and raising funds that it changed the church's focus.

The truth is the church already had plenty of room to grow. By adding a third worship service and adding Christian education classes at other times, the church could have grown to 1400 or 1500 in their existing building. Instead, the church decided to build, diverting the leaders' best creative energy to the building program even before the building began.

This changed focus was obvious within the congregation. When asked how the church was doing, members would describe how the building program was going and express impatience with the process. They honestly believed the church could not move ahead until the building was finished. The building program, rather than inspiring members to reach out, tended to put the church's ministries on hold.

Although the bigger building created the illusion of growth, in the twenty years since the building program, the congregation has not grown. For yet one more church, building a building had become an unfortunate substitute for the church's real work.

Losing Focus by Neglecting Ministry

The people of First Baptist Church in Brewster, New York, were immersed in meeting the needs of people in this New York City suburb. Church families had taken in homeless teens and single moms and their children. In a nearby house, the church provided food and shelter for street people. A group of believers had prayed that a bar and house of prostitution would be closed and the building would become available for the homeless. The business was soon forced to close over tax issues, and the owner offered to let the church use the building rent free. Their prayers were answered! First Baptist's total focus was on meeting the needs of people.

Not surprisingly, the church was growing, and they asked me to work with them to develop a remodeling plan to give them more room to grow. The plan was affordable and would not require any borrowing. As I discussed the plan with the pastor, I cautioned him on one point. "Paul," I said, "I know you have people in this congregation who have the skills to do this remodeling themselves.

Because you want to keep putting your funds into the ministries that have been so effective, it will be tempting to let your people do the remodeling. Don't let them. Hire someone to do it for you. Otherwise, the time and energy your people now put into caring for the homeless, for runaways, and for other displaced people will be diverted to the building. It will change your church's focus, and your ministry will suffer."

The church adopted my recommendations on every point but one: the people decided to do the remodeling themselves. Two years later I had lunch with that pastor. "Ray," he said, "you were right. We did the remodeling ourselves, and it changed our focus. We have almost recovered from that mistake, but still have not fully regained our momentum."

Losing Focus through Staff Burnout

We worked with the senior pastor of a large growing church who took on the responsibilities of directing a major building program while continuing to pastor. The pressures on him during those two and a half years of planning and construction were greater than anyone should be subjected to. This led to a breakdown of his physical, spiritual, and moral life. He lost his relationship with the church, his wife, and his family. I was the architect for more than one church where this happened. It happens far more often than we want to admit.

My best advice to pastors is this: you were called to be a pastor. If you believe you are now called to oversee building, then leave the pastorate, get training, and pursue that call. Never do both.

Few churches prepare adequately for the challenges of a building program. When building is the only way to provide space for growth, how can the church keep its focus on ministry? The answer is wise preparation.

1. Develop a clear ministry plan to be led by staff and ministry leaders who will not be involved in implementing the building program.

2. Appoint a team to direct the building program as their primary service to the church.

3. Do not allow any pastor to be in charge of any aspect of the building program except as an advisor. (An exception: an administrative or executive pastor who oversees facilities.)

4. Before committing to build, have in place a complete financial plan that meets the requirements in the financial section of this book. Eliminate surprises as much as possible.

5. Protect your focus on ministry by operating on provision, not debt.

With wise preparation, a healthy growing church can plan and pay for a building without ever taking its focus off meeting the needs of people.

Regaining Focus

Returning to Champlain's story, after twenty-nine years, the church leaders decided they were sick and tired of being a non-growing maintenance church. They added support staff, added signage to be more visitor-friendly, did some minor remodeling, and made more creative use of their space. They increased giving and expanded outreach ministries. The church gave the pastor a housing allowance, freeing up the parsonage next door to be converted to offices so the expanding staff could work as a team and be available to the community during the week.

How could they pay for all this? They had finally paid off their mortgage, ending their heavy burden of debt and enabling the church to return its focus to ministry once again.

Yes, building can kill a church's growth, but it doesn't have to. A growing church *can* plan and pay for a building program in such a way that the members never take their focus off meeting the needs of people. The way to accomplish this is neither difficult nor mysterious, as the following chapters show. It just calls for a bit of unconventional wisdom.

15

The Myth of Sacred Space

Ray: It was an architect's dream come true. First Church had the money to do it right. The building committee gave me the freedom to incorporate into the design everything I believed a sanctuary should be. This was the opportunity I'd been waiting for—the ultimate sanctuary.

I didn't have to think twice to know what I wanted to capture in that sanctuary's design. Years of architectural training, many more years of practical experience specializing in church architecture, and my own love for the beauty of the great historic sanctuaries—all of these had prepared me for this moment. I was ready.

I told the building committee what I had told dozens of building committees before: "The sanctuary is the heart of the church, a sacred space devoted exclusively to the worship of God. Building your sanctuary should take priority over all the church's building needs. Until you have such a sanctuary, the church's worship will never be all it should be."

The committee enthusiastically supported my proposal, and I set out to design the sanctuary of my dreams. My design would make people want to attend First Church. Once they were there, the environment would speak to their spirits. The stained glass, the pipe organ, the strong vertical lines, the dynamic symmetry—more than mere aesthetics, these design elements would draw people to God, inspire them to worship. And through worship they would be changed. No mere bricks and mortar, this building; no, it would be a means of grace.

My confidence in the power of architecture was hardly unusual. During my architectural training I had been taught, as most architects are, that the key to solving social problems was to create new and better environments in which to live, work, learn, and, in my case, worship. Though I would not discover it for several years, there was a problem with that belief: it was wrong.

That realization came gradually. A church in Nampa, Idaho, asked me to design a worship space for them with a multilevel platform, movable choir seats, portable risers, and ramps to make it easy to move props and equipment on and off stage. They envisioned using the space for dramas at Christmas and Easter, for a symphony orchestra, for big or small choirs that could be moved to various locations. While designing that sanctuary, cracks began to appear in my traditional thinking.

Three years later I designed my first totally flexible church facility. Worship, Sunday school, fellowship, and recreation all took place in the same area. The building had no "sacred space"—space set aside exclusively for worship. Though the congregation saw this building as temporary, to be replaced later by a single-use sanctuary, designing it opened my mind to new possibilities.

My traditional thinking was further challenged when I left my architectural firm to become a consultant. Because I wanted to help churches do facility planning in a biblical context, I spent a lot of time studying the New Testament. And what I found startled me.

First, I discovered that *sanctuary* is an Old Testament concept that was abolished in Christ. *Sanctuary* means "where God dwells," and in the Old Testament the Holy of Holies was indeed a special dwelling place for God. But when Jesus breathed his last on the cross, the curtain of the temple tore from top to bottom and opened the Holy of Holies—where God dwelled—to all humanity.

Scripture leaves no doubt about where God dwelled from that moment on:

> [God] doesn't live in man-made temples (Acts 17:24 NLT).
>
> Don't you realize that all of you together are the temple of God and that the Spirit of God lives in you? (1 Cor. 3:16 NLT).
>
> Your body is the temple of the Holy Spirit (1 Cor. 6:19 NLT).
>
> We are his house, built on the foundation of the apostles and the prophets. And the cornerstone is Christ Jesus himself. We are carefully joined together in him, becoming a holy temple for the Lord (Eph. 2:20–21 NLT).
>
> You are living stones that God is building into his spiritual temple (1 Pet. 2:5 NLT).

All my life I had heard that the church building, especially the sanctuary, was "God's house." Had I lived before Christ's earthly ministry, it might have been appropriate to give that kind of reverence to the temple. But my Bible study now convinced me that my thinking was two thousand years out of date. As Jesus explained to the woman at the well, it's not *where* we worship that counts, but *how* we worship (see John 4:21–24).

I realized no human could ever design a sanctuary.

For the first time I realized no human could ever design a sanctuary. No amount of money, no amount of stained glass or carpet or padded pews could transform bricks and mortar into the dwelling place of God. God has already chosen his dwelling place and he has chosen not "man-made temples" but the hearts of his people.

Second, my Bible study showed me that the New Testament church owned no church buildings, though they held both large-group and small-group meetings. The large-group gatherings, for the most part, were not meetings of the church—believers—but rather meetings for public evangelism. These took place in the temple courts, in a public market, in synagogues, in a rented hall, on a riverbank. The churches met in homes. It seems to have never crossed the apostles' minds that they might need to build large auditoriums.

In Jerusalem people came to Christ by the tens of thousands and possibly hundreds of thousands. Today such rapid growth would promptly run into obstacles. Where could we find facilities large enough for all those people to meet? Even the temple courts would have been quickly overrun had they all tried to meet together. But meeting space was no problem for those first Christians, because as more people became Christians, more homes—thousands of them—became available as meeting places.

The first-century church prayed, taught, evangelized, healed, baptized, ate together, celebrated the Lord's Supper, shared to meet the needs of others, sang, worshiped, and praised God. And they did it all without owning a single church building.

For almost three centuries the church built few if any buildings, and it continued to enjoy the most vigorous period of ministry and growth the church has ever known. Then disaster struck. Constantine declared Christianity the state religion. The church became less and less a community of believers and more and more a religious institution. The church built buildings and more buildings. Its focus had shifted. The church's most dynamic era had come to an end.

> **For almost three centuries the church built few if any buildings, and it continued to enjoy the most vigorous period of ministry and growth the church has ever known.**

Now, I know the gospel is supposed to be good news, but for an architect, especially one who had already invested most of a lifetime in designing church buildings, my biblical findings did not feel like good news. Had my decades of service to the church as an architect been wasted? Was the whole concept of a "church architect" inconsistent with a New Testament vision of church, a church without sanctuaries?

What would happen, I wondered, *if I left behind my arrogant belief that I could design a building that would draw people to*

God, cause them to worship, inspire them to change? What if I started with the idea that the church is people and its mission is to meet the needs of people in Christ's name? What kind of building would result?

To find an answer I looked to the words of Christ. I noticed that he continually described himself and his kingdom with words such as *meek*, *lowly*, *kind*, *merciful*, *good*, *just*, and *humble*. What kind of design would reflect these values?

Personally, I loved Gothic architecture with its ornate grandeur, but it clearly did not reflect the values of Jesus. Rather, it was a monument to the pride and power of humanity. A design based on Jesus's values would not be ornate but simple, not pretentious but restrained. The space would not overpower people with its lavishness or size but would make them feel welcome and comfortable. The very style of the architecture would say that the people are more important than the building.

I looked around at growing churches for clues. Most growing churches used their buildings differently from other churches. They held multiple worship services and Sunday schools. They used most rooms for multiple ministries. They had fewer classes on campus and more groups meeting in homes, offices, and restaurants.

I came to see that unbiblical attitudes toward church buildings were great barriers to ministry and church growth. This setting apart of "sacred space," intended as an expression of reverence, actually hinders the work of God. It often takes the church's focus off its mission as members divert time, money, and energy away from ministering to people and toward building and paying for unnecessary buildings.

I began to recommend a "ministry center," a large area with a level floor and movable furnishings that could be used not only for worship but also for a host of other ministry activities throughout the week.

Does this mean that every church should worship in multiuse space? No. Some churches don't need to use their worship center for other functions. Some have enough income to build a dedicated worship center along with other space for all other ministry needs.

The worship style in some liturgical churches makes it impractical to conduct worship in multiuse space. But whatever the cultural and worship needs of the church, the principle is the same: the building itself is not sacred. If the church's mission is to minister to people in Christ's name, church buildings can have only one legitimate function: to serve as tools to help Jesus's followers better fulfill that mission. If our focus is truly on people rather than buildings, that reality will shape the kinds of buildings we design, how we use them, how much we spend on them, and how much time, energy, and money we keep free for the real work of the church: meeting people's needs.

16

Three Things Church Buildings Can Never Do

Ray: If you had eavesdropped on a phone conversation in my office some years ago, you might have heard something like this:

"I'd like you to come talk to my board about a new building," the pastor said.

"That sounds good," I answered. "What do you need?"

"The people need a challenge. They haven't done anything for years, and a building program will wake them up and unite them behind a cause."

"You're right," I said. "Nothing is more exciting than building."

"There's a lot of money in our church," the pastor went on, "but giving has been going downhill lately. A new building will increase stewardship. If we plan a project for a million dollars, I think that will be enough to really challenge the people. I've decided to hire a professional fund-raiser to raise about a third of that amount through a three-year giving drive. We can borrow the rest."

"Will your regular income cover the payments?" I wanted to know.

"Not yet, but the new building should bring in new people, and the increased giving will cover the payments."

"That's exciting! With that kind of money we can design an award-winning structure that will put your church on the map, one the people of your community will want to attend. What kind of building do you need?"

"Well, we haven't grown for years, so our sanctuary is old and should make a good family life center. That should attract families. So I guess it's logical to build a new sanctuary."

"How many should we plan for?"

"We have around three hundred regular attenders, so we should plan for real growth—say eight hundred to one thousand."

"That should really give your people a vision of the possibilities and motivate them to reach out. When can we start?"

Though I'm not proud of it, I've had many conversations much like this one and passed along the same conventional wisdom I'd heard about building programs from countless pastors and church leaders. I now realize that this "conventional wisdom" includes many fallacies. When a church buys into these fallacies, disappointment and sometimes disaster result. Here are three of the most common and costly false expectations I am guilty of having promoted.

False: Building Will Stimulate Growth

When I designed my dream sanctuary for First Church (ch. 15), I fully expected the building to attract new people and make the church grow faster. It was the most architecturally perfect building I had ever designed. The congregation was united behind the building program, and there were no financial problems—nothing in the process to hinder growth. If ever one of my buildings was going to stimulate growth, this one would.

Several years after the building was complete, I charted the church's growth history. Before the building program, the church had been growing at a steady rate of 3 percent a year.

After the building program, the church had grown at 3 percent a year.

It was humbling for this architect to admit that no church building, however perfectly designed, can make a church grow. The most a building can do is *allow* a church to grow.

In one church of 160, those who "wanted the church to grow" were promoting a plan to relocate to a business district centrally located among the communities the church served. Relocation, they claimed, would make the church grow. "Our church is in an out-of-the-way place," they said. "Our building is full. The basement smells bad and there's nothing we can do about it. And we don't have enough parking."

Actually, none of that was true. They could double their parking simply by paving and marking the parking lot. All the basement needed was a good ventilation system. With creative planning, their building would give the congregation room to double before it needed to build. And their location was actually better than the one proposed for a new building.

While unattractive or inadequate facilities can hinder growth, for this church facilities were not the problem, they were an excuse. The real problem was that the church was doing absolutely nothing to grow. They didn't even follow up with guests.

Their attitude toward outreach was symbolized by two stern, silent old men who stood guard at the door. Though each wore a "greeter" badge, they looked more like people you might recruit to frighten children at a haunted house. When I visited their service, it was not until I greeted the "greeters" that either spoke to me. Though the congregation did not need a new building, some members preferred to promote a building program rather than do the work of outreach that could actually lead to growth.

False: Building Will Increase Giving to Ministry

The myth that building programs will motivate more giving to ministry is an especially dangerous one, because it often appears to be true. Building programs usually do motivate people to give. Especially at the beginning, large sums of money can be raised for a building program. A few members may even increase their giving long-term. So what's wrong with expecting a building program to increase giving to ministry?

The increased giving isn't going to ministry. Building buildings is not the work of the church. The work of the church is to meet people's needs. While a building program may motivate people to give more to pay for buildings, seldom is the increased giving enough to cover the cost of the building.

A rapidly growing church in Oklahoma earmarked 5 percent of all its income for local outreach. These funds were invested in various local ministries in which members of the church were involved, including an inner-city ministry, a ministry to pregnant teens, and several other ongoing projects.

When the congregation launched a multimillion-dollar building program, the people gave generously in response. However, when building costs exceeded estimates, the church began looking for places to cut expenses. They abandoned their earmarking of 5 percent for local outreach and redirected most of those funds to the building program. While total giving increased, funds directed to meeting the needs of people decreased.

False: Building Will Motivate People to Minister

One of the first churches I worked for as an architect was a congregation of fifty in a small Kansas town. The moment I saw their building I understood why they wanted to build. It was small, dark, and dilapidated. The members were embarrassed to invite their friends. I would have been embarrassed too. If only they had a new, attractive building, the leaders thought, the people would no longer be embarrassed and would reach out to the community.

I helped them design a building that gave them room to grow. It had a bright nursery, attractive Sunday school rooms, and plenty of parking. They built that building and opened the doors.

That was decades ago. Though the church has grown some, today it still has not outgrown that building. Why? After all, they did a lot of things right. They really did need a building, the building fit the congregation's needs, and its cost was reasonable.

This church's mistake was that they expected a building to motivate people to minister. The members did not have a passion to reach people before they built. A new building did nothing to change that.

These three false expectations have one thing in common: they all assume that buildings can meet non-building needs. Buildings cannot stimulate growth, inspire healthy stewardship, or motivate outreach. Why? Because these are all ministry needs, not building needs, and buildings cannot minister.

> **These three false expectations have one thing in common: they all assume that buildings can meet non-building needs.**

If buildings cannot minister, what purpose do they serve? They are *tools for ministry*. A wrench can't repair a faucet, and a word processor can't write a book, but they can help the plumber and the writer do their jobs better. In the same way, an appropriate building—whether borrowed, rented, or owned—can provide space well-suited to the ministries it serves. It can help people feel more comfortable and welcomed. It can provide workspace and equipment to increase efficiency. It can make the ministries of the church more accessible to the community. It can do all these and more.

But there is one thing a building can never do: it can never minister. Only people can do that.

Why Do You Want to Build?

Which of the following reasons to build are motivating your church's leaders to consider building? Check those that apply.

_____ 1. A new building will attract new people to the church.

_____ 2. A new location and/or higher visibility will enhance our growth.

_____ 3. Members will be more motivated to reach out to others once we have a new building.

_____ 4. A new sanctuary used only for worship will make our services more effective and inspire people to worship.

_____ 5. A building program will involve more people in the work of the church.

_____ 6. A building program will motivate our people to give more generously to the work of the church.

_____ 7. A building program will unify our people behind a significant challenge.

_____ 8. A new building will increase interest in the church and give the church greater status in the community.

_____ 9. Our people will take greater pride in their church when the new building is complete.

_____ 10. A new building will allow all of our people to worship in a single service.

_____ 11. A new facility will provide our people with a more effective tool for ministry.

Interpreting Your Answers

All eleven of these reasons for building are common, but most are not adequate reasons to build. Statements 1 through 4 express the expectation that the building will minister. Attracting new people to the church ("build it and they will come"), motivating members to reach out, and inspiring worship are all important goals for the church, but they are all ministry goals.

Statements 5 through 7 assume that building buildings is the work of the church, or at least integral to the church's work; therefore, when people unite behind a building program by giving their time, money, or energy to it, they are doing the work of the church. This common attitude, however, is simply unbiblical. When a church builds for any of these reasons, building has become an unfortunate substitute for the real work of the church.

Statements 8 and 9 express worldly values that often creep into the church. The notion that bigger and better buildings are symbols of prestige or success is unworthy of a church that is called to reject materialism and be a servant people.

Building so your church can go back to—or remain in—a single service (statement 10) grows out of a valid desire for community, but it approaches that need in a way that normally hinders growth. Unless your church has decided that you do not want to reach more people, this is almost never a valid reason to build.

Statement 11, building to provide church members with a more effective tool for ministry, is the only motivation for building consistent with the church's purpose. If the church regards buildings as tools and nothing more, this will guide the decision not only of *whether* to build but *how* to build. A building designed to serve will look very different from one designed to impress.

If you checked any of the first ten statements, your church needs to further clarify its motives for building before it moves ahead. Failing to do so will almost certainly bring disappointing results.

If you checked only statement 11, congratulations! You have passed the motivation test, the first of three tests your church must pass to be ready to build.

The Principle of Use

A church needs more space only when it
is fully utilizing the space it already has.

17

Teaching Old Church Buildings New Tricks

Before your car comes to a complete stop, your fourteen-year-old son jumps out and sprints to the youth building to join his Sunday school class. For the nearly one hundred years since your original church building was built, the youth had been meeting in a concrete-block basement classroom, so when the church built a steel building last year and promised the youth group it would be all theirs—no one else could use it—your son and the twenty other middle and high school students were pumped! Hoping to attract more youth, some board members dream of building a gym to launch a recreation ministry.

You enter the church through the twenty-five-year-old education wing. You drop off your two younger children at the room where the elementary-age children gather in a large group for the first twenty minutes of Sunday school before going to their classrooms, then go on to your own class in the basement. You've been going to the same class for twelve years. You would love to start a new class for young marrieds who aren't plugging into any of the older classes. Your pastor is all for it, but all the classrooms are full. It will have to wait. As your class gathers, you hear the worship band starting to practice in the sanctuary above you.

After class you head upstairs for the worship service. The stairways and hallways are no wider than they were when the original building was built in the 1920s when attendance was half of what it is now. People love to complain about the traffic congestion, but no one really gets too upset about it.

At the top of the stairs you merge with those arriving through the main entrance who are being funneled through a tiny foyer into the rear of the sanctuary. The pews are about two-thirds full as you enter. By the time service begins, there are no easy-to-reach seats left for latecomers. For fifteen years people have been talking about building a bigger sanctuary. In fact, ten years ago plans were drawn up, but the price tag was so high that the plans have been collecting dust. Ever since your new pastor came three years ago, he has been reminding you that your church can't grow until you make room for more people. Everyone agrees, but they don't agree on what to do about it.

After the worship service everyone heads to the fellowship hall for a potluck meal held in honor of a couple's fortieth wedding anniversary.

Just off the fellowship hall next to a side entrance you see the newly remodeled offices—one for the secretary and one for the pastor. When the new pastor came, he moved his office from the room beside the stage and hired a professional full-time secretary. As wonderful as it has been to have professional offices, you lost a couple of classrooms in the bargain, and a few people are still grumbling about it.

When the new youth building opened, the church hired one of the youth sponsors as quarter-time student ministries director. Her office is in the youth building. Your minister of music, who works eight hours a week, has an office in the choir room just below the stage. Your pastor wants to hire an associate pastor. He says that you won't grow beyond two hundred until you expand your staff. No one knows, though, where you would put another office, much less where you would put more people. As the chair of the property committee likes to say, "We are fully using every square inch of this building for ministry and that is how it should be!"

There is only one problem with that observation: it's not true. In fact, almost every room in this building is underutilized.

Single-Use Architecture

Most older church buildings were designed to function like the one we just walked through. Each room was designed for one purpose. It was used for that purpose an hour or two, or maybe three, each week, and sat empty the rest of the time.

- The sanctuary is used for worship.
- The fellowship hall is used for meals.
- The classrooms are used for classes.
- The youth building or room is used for the youth group.
- The gym is used for recreation.

When any one part of the building is being used, most of the rest of the building is sitting empty. Even when the children gather as a large group, their classrooms are empty, and when they go to their classrooms, their large group room is empty.

A church that clings to single-use architecture will only be able to sustain growth when it can afford to build bigger buildings. Since new buildings are expensive, many churches will just stop growing, and those that can build will grow for a season then run into a wall and stop again.

Multiple-Use Design

If you don't want your single-use building to become a barrier to reaching new people, you can teach your old church building new tricks. Most new church buildings don't use single-use but rather multiple-use architecture. They are designed for multiple worship services and multiple sessions of Sunday school. Almost every space in the building is designed as multiple-use space. A single room may be set up in a half-dozen different ways for a half-dozen different kinds of ministry throughout the week.

Older church buildings were not designed to be used this way. When a church whose building was designed for single services decides to add a second service, it poses challenges. Passageways may be too narrow. The building may not have a fellowship foyer located in the right place where people leaving the first service can mingle with those arriving for the second service. The new schedule may create parking challenges.

Many older church buildings have rows of small classrooms. While this can work fairly well in small churches, medium and large churches need more flexible space.

While most churches of over 150 now have multiple staff, most older church buildings were not designed for multiple staff. Even if there are multiple offices, rarely is the office area designed to maximize collaboration within the staff team.

> **A church that clings to single-use architecture will only be able to sustain growth when it can afford to build bigger buildings. Since new buildings are expensive, many churches will just stop growing, and those that can build will grow for a season then run into a wall and stop again.**

Of course, older campuses also weren't designed to accommodate multivenue or multisite worship.

Multiplying Your Facility's Capacity

The people of the church we just walked through may think they are out of room. The good news is that they can multiply their capacity for a fraction of the cost of a new worship center. This building was originally designed to accommodate a congregation of 150. By adding an education wing and youth building and filling up every space, they have grown to two hundred. But they will not grow beyond two hundred until they increase their seating capacity, and the idea of a new sanctuary is intimidating. What else can they do to increase the capacity of their building?

1. *They can add a second service.* This is not as simple as scheduling a new service and launching it. Many second services fail, and for predictable reasons. Also, since older church buildings are not designed for multiple services, they often need at least modest remodeling. Chapter 18 shows you how to add a second (and third) service without repeating six common mistakes.

2. *They can redesign classrooms and change how they use them.* Larger, multiple-use classrooms; multiple sessions of classes; transitioning from solo teaching to team-teaching; streamlining children's programming to increase excellence; rethinking discipleship strategies for adults and students—these changes can multiply growth capacity with little or no additional square footage while increasing ministry effectiveness. Chapter 19 describes ways to accomplish this.

3. *They can create a new office suite.* Most churches underestimate the strategic importance of great offices. Scattered, cramped, inefficient offices waste staff members' time (and so waste staff dollars) and sabotage collaboration. For a building designed for 150 to be repurposed to serve a congregation of four hundred requires creating new offices. In fact, in teaching old church buildings new tricks, offices are often the first priority for new construction. You can triple the size of your congregation without tripling the size of your worship center, classrooms, fellowship hall, or parking, but you cannot do it without tripling your staff and giving them offices. Designing great offices is the subject of chapter 20.

4. *They can add another worship venue and perhaps eventually another campus.* This church of two hundred can create the space to grow to four hundred by implementing the three strategies above. At that point, depending on the limitations of their facility and site, they may be able to continue to grow in the same facility by adding a second worship venue. If this

is feasible, it could enable them to grow to as many as six hundred in a building originally designed for 150. At that point, with the financial resources of a larger congregation, the church might be ready to build a new building. Or they might find that it is more strategic and cost-effective to open a second campus in rented or repurposed space. Chapter 21 explores these options.

A church that thought it was "using every available square inch" actually had so much underutilized capacity that by changing programming and scheduling, remodeling, and making a modest addition or two, it had room to double, perhaps even triple, its weekend attendance. The next four chapters show you how to teach your old church building (or even your new one) these new tricks.

18

Adding a New Service

Six Common Mistakes to Avoid

When attendance reached 150 at Newton Christian Church (NCC) in Kansas, they either had to increase capacity or stop growing. They couldn't afford to build, but adding a second service didn't seem promising either. Why not? Because "we tried that and it didn't work."

Though multiple services have become common, they still have a high failure rate. Many churches run into serious problems when they add a second service. With rare exceptions, however, returning to one service is a step backward, triggering on average a 15 percent drop in attendance. The way forward is to learn to do multiple services well.

Twenty-four of NCC's leaders gathered and together went through the six common mistakes to avoid when starting a new service. They laughed nervously as they realized they had managed to make five of the six. By the end of the meeting, though, they were all ready to try again, confident they could avoid their previous mistakes.

Your church doesn't have to remake all the usual mistakes. You can learn from others' mistakes so your new service succeeds on the first try.

1. Having too little connections time.

The number one complaint about multiple services is, "We don't see our friends who attend the other service." This issue is critical, and if you don't address it effectively, your new service will likely either fail or leave a bitter taste in many mouths.

The good news is that you can add a second service in a way that lets people connect *more*, not less, with those who attend the other service.

> **You can add a second service in a way that lets people connect *more*, not less, with those who attend the other service.**

The key is an intentional connections time when people from the two services connect with one another and, just as importantly, with guests.

An effective connections time has four elements: time, space, food, and a ministry team.

- *Time.* You need twenty-five to forty minutes where people leaving the first service can connect with those arriving for the second service. If this time is too short, people won't have enough time to visit. If it is too long, people attending the first service will leave before people arrive for the second one. This means scheduling the two services just twenty-five to thirty minutes apart. Having Sunday school between services sabotages the connections time.[1]

- *Space.* Your connections area needs to be big enough that people can visit without feeling like they are blocking traffic. Otherwise, they will leave. Ideally, this area will be 50 to 60 percent of the square footage of your worship center. If your foyer isn't this big—and most foyers in older buildings are not—you will need to get creative. Possible solutions include expanding your foyer, using the back of your auditorium as a connections space, extending your connections area into the outdoors, and adding on.

The right place for your connections area is between your worship center(s) and the most-used entrances. Why? Because a key purpose of this ministry is to connect with guests. Unless guests have to pass through your connections area to get to and from worship, few will go out of their way to find it.

- *Food.* Nothing encourages conversation like food. In designing your connections time, a key goal should be to get a cup of coffee in the hand of each guest. Once people are holding drinks or snacks, they have given you permission to engage in conversation. People will stand—or sit—and visit longer if they are eating and drinking. You need some seating to make your connections time family-friendly, but people will interact more if most of them are walking around.

- *Hosts.* An effective connections time is a high-priority ministry, not simply "the time between services." Its purpose is to encourage relationships between those who attend the first and second services and to increase interaction with guests. Its success depends mainly on your team of hosts, whose ministry is to make newcomers feel welcome and to connect them to others with shared interests.

With a well-planned connections time, people attending different services will have more time to connect with each other than they did before.

2. Scheduling a too-early service.

Faith Tabernacle had Sunday school from 9:30 to 10:30 and traditional worship from 10:45 to 12:00. When they added a contemporary service from 8:00 to 9:15, it attracted mostly younger families. However, quite a few younger families kept coming to the second service mainly because it was hard to get the kids ready by 8:00. Five years after the new service launched, it was still only half the size of the traditional service.

Many churches that run into this problem reverse the order of the services after a couple of years, realizing that the later time works better for young families and many older adults prefer the earlier time.

An even better solution is to start the whole morning later by holding two sessions of Sunday school and/or children's church simultaneous with the worship services with a thirty-minute connections time between. The schedule looks something like this:

9:00–10:15	Worship and Sunday school/children's church
10:15–10:45	Connections time
10:45–12:00	Worship and Sunday school/children's church

In most communities, moving the early service from 8:00 to 9:00 leads to higher attendance.

3. Having energy-draining empty seats.

When a church launches a second service, it can trade in one growth barrier, overcrowding, for another, the empty-room syndrome. People who are scattered throughout the auditorium visit less with other worshipers. Because they can't hear others singing nearby, they feel like they are singing alone and their singing is timid. When visitors enter a mostly empty room, they wonder, *Where is everybody? What's wrong?* A mostly empty room turns many worshipers into passive observers.

Depending on the shape of your room and what kind of seating you have, a room feels crowded when 70 to 85 percent of the seating is full. Most rooms feel empty whenever the seating is less than half full.

How do you fix this? Set up the right number of seats for each service. If you expect about 125 people, set up 150 to 175 chairs. If you expect 300, set up 375 to 400 chairs.

What if you have pews? There are several possible solutions.

- Often the best answer is to replace your pews with high-quality worship chairs. For each service, set up the number needed. If the chairs fill up, your ushers set up more chairs.
- Hold one service in another room where you can set up the right number of chairs.
- Remove several pews from the back of the auditorium. Use the open space for your connections time and for additional seating when attendance is high.
- Block off the back pews with portable screens. While less than ideal, this works better than roping off pews. (Ropes dare people to climb over them!)

A key to making space feel full: empty space *behind* worshipers usually doesn't make the room feel empty. The problem is the empty seats people see.

If you have a small group in a large space—fifty people, for example, meeting in a gym—you can use dividers or furniture to create a smaller space.

Creative use of lighting and sound can also shrink a room. Lighting just one section of a big room makes the space feel smaller. Adjusting or upgrading your sound system so that all parts of the room are filled with sound makes the room feel more full.

4. Overextending leaders.

Launching a second service without first expanding leadership capacity burns out leaders. Adding a second service usually increases worship preparation time beyond what a volunteer can handle. If you don't have a paid worship team leader when you transition to multiple worship services, consider adding a part-time position.

Adding a second service normally adds complexity to your children's programming. Some churches need to add a part-time staff member to handle increased administration for two sessions of children's ministry.

You will need greeters, ushers, and hosts for your connections time for two services.

And, of course, the pastor has to plan two services and preach twice, which takes time and energy. What will you take off your pastor's plate to offset this increased workload? (If your services are identical, the increased load for the pastor and musicians is far less than if you have two styles of worship.)

Before launching a second service, you need to have all these bases covered.

5. Creating a second-class second service.

Many second services fail because they are second class. People attending the new service feel like they are missing the main event. There are many ways to signal that a service is second class:

- The best music is in the "main" service, not the new service.
- Most baptisms, baby dedications, and welcoming of new members happen in the other service.
- The new service doesn't provide a nursery.
- The children's ministry for the new service is weaker than that offered for the other service.
- Those attending the new service have fewer adult education options than those attending the other service.
- The schedule makes it inconvenient for early worshipers to attend after-church dinners.
- One service remains at the old time; the new service is at a new time. (A better solution is for both services to meet at new times.)

The services may be identical or different. The key is that people see the services as equally important and valuable in accomplishing the church's mission.

6. Having just-until-we-build expectations.

Some growing churches add a second service to buy time until they can build a bigger auditorium and all meet together again.

Approaching a second service as a just-until-we-build stopgap sets the second service up for failure. When you present it as temporary, the church is not likely to make the investments in connections time, creative scheduling, optimal seating arrangements, leadership capacity, children's ministry, or music that would make the service thrive long term.

We typically don't advise building a larger worship center until the church is nearing capacity in at least three services and two or three sessions of Sunday school. Even then, building a bigger worship auditorium is just one of five options we explore, and usually it's not the best one.[2]

When a second service has failed for whatever reasons, it is sometimes wise to go back to one service for a while so the church can correct its mistakes, and then launch a new service on sound footing. The key is for the *single* service to be seen as *temporary* and for multiple services to be viewed as the norm.

Newton Christian Church identified the mistakes they had made the first time they added a second service. They formed a connections team, developed a plan for optimal seating, ramped up the leadership on their worship and children's ministry teams, and cast a vision for multiple services as a long-term strategy. After four months of planning they launched their new service. As is typical, within a month their attendance jumped 15 percent. Over the next eighteen months, their attendance grew by 50 percent.

Adding a Third Service

Adding a third service is both easier and harder than adding the second. The hardest part of adding a second service is overcoming the expectation that everyone should worship together. You don't have to cross that bridge again when you add the third. The logistics of adding a third service, however, are more complex.

What key decisions do you have to make in launching a third service?

- *What will your schedule be?* Will your three services be consecutive, or will you have two Sunday morning services and the third another day or time?
- *What service times will work best for the demographic each service is designed to reach?* For example, an early morning service may work fine for seniors, but not for college students or families with young children.

> **The easiest way to staff for children's ministries is for people to attend one service and serve during another.**

- *How will you structure connections times between services?*
- *How will you organize your volunteer teams—children's ministry, worship, guest services (greeters/ushers/ food team/parking/connections time hosts)?* Will they be scheduled vertically (working all three services in one weekend a month) or horizontally (serving during a single service every week)?
- *How will you staff?* Will you need more staff for music/ worship? For children or youth? Support staff to lighten the load of equipping staff that will have more responsibilities?
- *How will you cast vision?*

Before Riverside added their third service, they talked with more than thirty churches that had three or more services. Some interviews were by phone, others at conferences, and still others onsite. A few key learnings:

- Follow the "attend one, serve one" principle. Normally, the easiest way to staff for children's ministries is for people to attend one service and serve during another. When the third service is not consecutive with the other two, "attend one, serve one" doesn't work well and the church typically struggles to get enough volunteers. Because of this, some churches add their third and fourth services at the same time, for example, at 4:00 and 6:00 on Saturday, so workers can come to one service and serve during the other.

An exception: we worked with a church in Austin, Texas, that had a stand-alone third service on Sunday evenings for families worshiping together, preceded by a family meal. Because there were no separate family ministries to staff (except nursery), it worked great!

- If you have the same style of music in all your worship services, worship teams serve vertically. That is, the same band plays in all three services, and then doesn't play again until two, three, or four weeks later. This helps all services to be seen as equally important.

- Most children's workers are generally scheduled horizontally, serving every Sunday during the same time period. Why? Because consistency of relationships between the workers and the children is at the heart of discipling children. Other workers—worship leaders, storytellers, and so forth—may serve on a monthly rotation.

- The most important challenge of all is to cast a vision for reaching more people. Leaders have to create a culture among all volunteers that reaching more people really matters.

A year after launching their third service, Riverside's attendance has increased 20 percent, and more than 20 percent of the worshipers are attending the third service. They are getting ready to launch a second campus with two services. Why? Because, as they say at Riverside, "Lost people matter to God."

19

More-with-Less
Classroom Strategies

A church in South Hutchinson, Kansas, was considering building a classroom addition, but when they took a closer look, they discovered they already had room to add five more classes.

First Presbyterian Church in Warsaw, Indiana, asked their planner to design an addition with five large adult classrooms. But once they identified their most effective strategy for discipling adults, the need for those classrooms disappeared.

In Wichita, Kansas, a church that said they were out of classroom space looked at their building through new eyes and discovered they were using less than half of their available space.

A Muskegon, Michigan, church that needed more room for children and youth was struggling to find an affordable solution. A change in teaching methods, together with reconfiguring their existing space, gave them plenty of room to grow.

A church in Butler, Pennsylvania, was thinking of building a new building to give their midweek children's program room to grow. After clarifying their ministry goals, they realized that expanding that program would actually make ministry less, not more, effective.

> **Most churches that think they need more classrooms have better, less costly ways to meet their space needs.**

Whenever you have trouble finding space for a group to meet, it is natural to jump to the conclusion, "We need more classrooms." But as the experience of these churches—and thousands more—shows, most churches that think they need more classrooms have better, less costly ways to meet their space needs. Here are a few tried and proven more-with-less strategies.

Reclaim Wasted Space

A church with room to spare expands to fill the available space. Then if the church grows, it feels like they are out of room when in reality there is a lot of wasted space that can be reclaimed.

- *Storage.* Do you have a classroom—or parts of classrooms—being used for storage? Some churches can free up half their storage space with a trip to the city dump. Are you fully utilizing attic storage? A garage or storage shed? You can build an unheated storage shed or addition for a fraction of the cost of a classroom addition.

- *Oversize furnishings.* Some churches "collect" hand-me-down couches, overstuffed chairs, and pianos that are rarely played. If you are tight on space, get rid of these, then become really good at saying "no thanks" to offers of space-eating hand-me-downs. Slides and jungle gyms can be great fun in the nursery, but they only make sense if you have lots of space to spare. A church with a cramped foyer increased its foyer capacity by one third without spending a penny by removing the pews, communion table, and other furniture that had somehow become a part of the foyer landscape.

- *Right-size rooms.* Do you have a couple of classes bursting at the seams while others use only a fourth of the room? Move big classes to big rooms and small classes to small rooms.

Don't permit adult classes to "own" a room. Reassign rooms each year—or more often as needed—based on class size.

- *No more single-use rooms.* The church in South Hutchinson had a quilting room that was used just once a week for quilting. They realized they could use it for a class on Sunday. Their library was also empty on Sunday. The office reception area was empty on Sunday and had plenty of room for a class. With portable dividers, a corner of the foyer could easily be used for a class. As a general rule, you can design all your rooms, except restrooms and some offices, as multiuse space.

- *The "opening exercise" room.* Many small churches have a big room for opening exercises for children, and smaller rooms for Sunday school classes. When the large room is full, the small rooms are empty; when the small rooms are full, the large room is empty. At any given time, half the space is wasted. To fully use this space—and double your capacity—use the opening exercise space as a large, open classroom for at least half of your children. Use lightweight, adjustable-height tables so workers can convert the room from row seating for opening exercises to table seating in a minute or two.

Rethink Your Adult Discipleship Model

In itemizing the needs they wanted their facility plan to address, the vision committee of First Presbyterian Church in Warsaw, Indiana, said they wanted five more classrooms so they could expand their adult Sunday school from five classes to ten. Their goal was to involve all the adults in their church in a Sunday school class.

Gus, the director of Christian education, explained that lack of space wasn't their only barrier to growing the adult Sunday school. He was also having trouble recruiting teachers, and the adults not attending adult Sunday school showed little interest in starting.

Ron, the associate pastor who oversaw home-based small-group ministries, had run into the same problems—a shortage of leaders and a lack of interest among potential participants.

When asked to name the primary ministry goal of adult Sunday school and small groups, Gus immediately identified fellowship as the major purpose of both. Which ministry setting served that ministry purpose more effectively? Without hesitation, Gus said "small groups." These two programs were trying to meet the same need, competing for the same participants and leaders. That was why both programs had stalled out halfway to their goal.

First Presbyterian decided to make small groups their primary setting for community-building and adult disciple-making. This meant redefining the purpose of adult Sunday school, placing less emphasis on relationship building in class groups and more emphasis on teaching with short-term electives. All adults would be encouraged to meet every week with their home-based small groups and to take elective classes on Sundays only as they had time and interest—not fifty-two weeks a year. If some adults, particularly older adults, preferred to continue to relate to their Sunday school class as a small group, that would be great. But they wouldn't be expected to also join a weekday small group. These redefined expectations meant the church didn't need more adult classes, so the need for five new classrooms disappeared.

The pastor of Stillmeadow Nazarene Church in York, Pennsylvania, told his people, "Being part of this church means being involved in a face-to-face discipleship group." He went on to describe different kinds of small groups they could choose to join—Sunday school classes, men's groups, women's groups, couples' groups, and more. Then he said, "We want each of you to be involved in one of these groups, but we don't want any of you to be involved in more than one. Why not? Because if people are involved in more than one, it stretches our leadership too thin, and we are committed to excellence in leadership." Because most discipleship groups met in homes, restaurants, or at the church during the week, the church only needed a couple of adult classrooms.

To accommodate their rapid growth over the past nine years, on Sundays Riverside dedicates almost all its classroom space to children. Its adult groups—Bible studies, men's groups, women's

groups, recovery groups, GriefShare, Financial Peace University—
all meet at other times or places.

Switch to Team-Teaching

A Wichita, Kansas, church felt like they had no growing room
because every classroom was being used. When they realized that
only a couple of rooms were full and most were only a quarter
to half full, they came up with new ways to use their space. They
combined several small children's classes into a larger team-taught
class with interest centers throughout the room—an approach the
teachers had used and loved in vacation Bible school. They suddenly had empty classrooms, but more importantly, both children
and teachers found the new format more engaging.

The entire basement of the Muskegon church was divided
into small children's classrooms, with no more rooms available
for growth. Their solution was to remove all the basement walls
and divide the entire basement into two large rooms, one for the
younger elementary grades and one for the older grades. The large
open spaces were ideal for active play during their Wednesday night
program. When Sunday classes met, supply cabinets on casters were
rolled out of a storage room to serve as dividers. Without adding a
single square foot, their children's ministry went from being maxed
out to having room to grow by 60 percent.

Refocus Weekday Programming

In Butler, Pennsylvania, the midweek children's program was bursting at the seams. The program leaders got together to weigh their
options. The obvious solution was to construct another building so
the program could grow. Most of the workers, though, confessed
that they were already overwhelmed with the number of children
in the program without adding any more. "I don't even know the
names of all the children in my group," one worker said.

The stated purpose of the program was to build bridges to families without church homes, but everyone agreed that none of the workers had the time to build relationships with parents. They had their hands more than full just trying to run the program. Growing the program larger, they realized, would only make the problem worse. They didn't need another building; they needed to cap enrollment in the program at a level that would make quality relationships with children and parents possible.

A church in Indiana started a preschool primarily as a way to build relationships with families who did not have church homes. It had grown into the largest preschool in town, with 250 students. Because they had children on the waiting list, the staff assumed they needed to build more classrooms. But, as with the Pennsylvania church, the preschool had grown beyond the staff's capacity to build quality relationships with all the children and their families. The preschool director agonized that the pressure of managing so many students was robbing her of the opportunity to build deeper relationships with the students and their parents. So, rather than building more classrooms and adding more students, the staff decided to focus more on depth of ministry than scope of ministry. The decision to not build freed the director to invest more time in building bridges between parents of preschoolers and church families, giving her new hope and lifting a huge burden from her.

When a church operates a school, preschool, or daycare center, there is the risk of the school becoming the tail that wags the dog. Schools can take on a life of their own, growing to fill space needed for the church's weekday ministries. Some schools are so heavily subsidized by the church that the church cannot afford to staff for growth.

If a church-operated school or daycare center is financially self-supporting, and the school itself can afford a new building, it may make sense to build. In over thirty years of working with churches, we have yet to find one where it was cost-effective for the church itself to build just to accommodate weekday ministries.

Implement Multiple Sessions

Just as you can increase worship seating capacity by adding services, you can increase classroom capacity by adding sessions. In fact, because of the importance of the connections time between services, when churches add a second service we normally recommend going to two sessions of classes at the same time. This suggestion is often met with horror: "But we are having trouble staffing one session; we could never come up with twice as many teachers!"

Done correctly, though, this isn't an issue. Two sessions of classes take about the same number of workers as a single session. Here's how it works.

Adult classes choose whether they prefer to meet first session or second. Ideally, you want about the same number of adult classes in each session. If, for example, your church has six adult classes, if three meet during each session you only need three adult classrooms, and three classrooms are freed up for other uses.

> **Done correctly, two sessions of classes take about the same number of workers as a single session.**

Youth meet all together in either the first or second session.

Nursery and preschool are probably already being provided during both your worship service and Sunday school hour, so this continues as it was before.

Classes for elementary-age children may require some restructuring. If you already have children's Sunday school during one hour and children's church during your service, you can continue something similar during your two worship services. If you are moving to a schedule where some children go to one session and some to the other, follow the principle that having multiple sessions doesn't change the worker-to-children ratio. For example, if you have forty elementary children, and after going to two sessions, you have twenty-five in the first session and fifteen in the second, your need for workers won't increase but you will need to restructure your groups. If, for example, you now have a class for each grade, you won't duplicate that in each session. Instead, in the first session you might have two team-taught classes and in the second session you might have all the children in one group where you use a broadly graded children's church curriculum. If you transition to a large-group team-teaching approach when you go to two sessions, you may, in fact, need fewer, not more, workers. Plus, recruiting workers for team-teaching is generally easier than recruiting for small classes. (See "The More We Teach Together" at the close of this chapter.)

Many churches with two services encourage their people to "attend one, serve one"—attend one worship service and serve in children's ministry or the connections ministry during the other service.

When you add a third worship service, it is ideal to add a third session of children's ministry so a lack of children's ministry doesn't hinder the growth of the new service.

While most small and medium churches have classes for children, youth, and adults on Sunday morning, larger, fast-growing churches tend to need most or all of their classrooms for children's ministry. Typically, youth worship with adults and have youth programming at another time. Adult discipleship takes place primarily in home-based groups, though there may be a few classes on Sundays such as a new members' class or a senior adult class.

By putting these five strategies to work, your church may be able to double or even triple your attendance before you need to add more classroom space.

─── **The More We Teach Together** ───

When Delora agreed to teach third-grade Sunday school at Faith Lutheran in Derby, Kansas, she said yes, but on one condition: "It's one year at a time." After a year, she quit. Why? "I had such high expectations of myself that it was exhausting to meet them," she said.

Delora is neither underqualified (professionally she teaches fifth grade in a private school) nor is she a victim of unrealistically high expectations. In fact, today she is teaching Sunday school again and says, "I can't tell you how much fun it is!"

What's made the difference? Team-teaching.

Every summer thousands of churches scramble to find enough teachers for fall Sunday school. As tempting as it is to blame this annual frustration on low commitment, the real culprit may be how we structure our classes.

Solo teaching with small classes, our most common way of conducting Sunday school, can make teaching children a lot harder—and less effective—than it needs to be. A team approach, where each ministry team works with a larger group of children, can bring out the best in children's workers and make children's ministry far more rewarding and effective. Here's why.

Team-teaching empowers every team member to minister out of his or her spiritual gifts.

Almost every church has a few teachers who can make the Bible come alive for children, but probably none can unearth a master teacher for every small children's class. Some people are great at leading children in worship. Others are gifted with leading activities or memory work. Rarely is any one person good at all these things, yet we expect solo teachers to do them all. Should we be surprised, then, when teachers feel overwhelmed?

Delora's three-member team teaches twenty to thirty fourth- through sixth-graders. Phyllis is great with pencil and paper games. David comes up with creative role plays. Delora shines at physical play. "I learn so much from watching how my teammates teach," Delora says. When every member of the team is ministering out of his or her gifts, ministry is more fun and more effective.

Team-teaching cuts preparation time.

One approach to team-teaching is for a master teacher to do all the preparation and for the other team members to assist. It's a lot easier to find people who enjoy working as caregivers than it is to recruit solo teachers.

Another system is to divide preparation among team members. At Hope Mennonite in Wichita, after a large-group opening the primary class breaks into three smaller groups. Each group goes to one of three activity centers. After ten minutes, the children rotate to different centers. Each worker leads the same activity three times with a different group of children. Each teacher needs only one-third the preparation time he or she needed under the old system.

Team-teaching builds in support.

Four years ago, when Faith Lutheran collected the teacher feedback forms after its vacation Bible school, teacher after teacher wrote, "I'll never do this again." Something had to change. The next year, the

VBS directors decided to try team-teaching. Several new VBS workers enjoyed it so much they volunteered to work regularly in Sunday school. In fact, since starting teaching teams in Sunday school, Faith has had almost no teacher turnover. "Phyllis thought about quitting," Delora says, "but it looks like she probably won't because of her friendships with the team."

Team-teaching requires fewer workers.

Consider, for example, a church that averages twenty-four children in grades 1–3—a first grade class of four students, and second- and third-grade classes of ten students each. To have one teacher for every six students, this department needs five teachers (one for grade 1, and two each for grades 2 and 3), plus a primary department supervisor—a total of six workers.

With a team approach, the work can be done, and done more effectively, by four workers and still provide the needed one to six ratio. Since each ministry team has internal leadership, no separate department supervisor is needed. In this way, one church was able to free up seven key leaders to minister in other ways.

Team-teaching helps with the substitute problem.

If one team member has to be gone one Sunday, the others may feel able to carry on without a substitute for one day. Or if a substitute is called in, he or she won't have to do any preparation.

Even more important is the impact on students. The heart of children's ministry isn't the printed curriculum, but the loving relationship between teachers and students through which a Christlike life is modeled. A team guarantees that students will be with teachers they know well even when one team member is away.

Team-teaching models Christian community.

As children watch adults ministering as a team, they learn more about how God designed the body of Christ to work than they can learn from any Bible lesson on body life. As they watch mature Christians love, support, and forgive each other, they learn what it means to live in Christian community.

Team-teaching reduces discipline problems.

Disruptive children can drive teachers away because they are so exhausting. Delora has found that team-teaching has solved this problem in her class. "We take turns teaching the lesson," she explains. "When David or Phyllis is teaching, I sit in the circle on the floor with the other students. For that week, I am a student, not a teacher. Sometimes I sit beside a student who needs extra attention, but by being part of the class I become a friend with these children. Because we're relating as friends, the disruptive behavior has practically disappeared."

As a bonus, team-teaching saves money on facilities.

Large-group team-teaching uses space more efficiently than small-group solo teaching. Olivet Evangelical Free Church in Muskegon, Michigan, needed growing room for their children's and teens' Sunday school classes. They considered building a three-thousand-square-foot youth building, but discovered that even that wouldn't meet their needs.

The solution they finally came up with was to tear out all their interior basement walls to eliminate their little classrooms and create a few large open areas—one for grades 1–3, one for grades 4–6, and one for teens. They would reconfigure their small classes into larger team-taught groups meeting in flexible, multipurpose space. Each space would have multiple work stations so students could work in smaller groups as appropriate. All furnishings would be portable, with a room for active storage nearby, so the space could also be used at other times for larger-scale activities such as recreation.

Remodeling their basement and switching to team-teaching will give Olivet's children's and teens' classes room to grow by 60 to 70 percent for a fraction of the cost of new construction.

If team-teaching is new to your church, how can you introduce it? By experimenting. Almost every teacher who gets a taste of team-teaching will jump at the chance to do it regularly. Try it out in vacation Bible school or a weeknight activity program. Or introduce it in one or two classes and let everyone see how it works before suggesting the whole children's department take the plunge.

What you'll discover, I suspect, is that the more we teach together, the more rewarding and effective our ministry with children will be.

20

Three Things Great Church Offices Do

Ray: To reach the church secretary's office, I had to enter the front door, pass through the auditorium, climb the stairs, go through the balcony, and finally open the door into the bell tower. The other offices were equally well hidden. The pastor's office was in the far corner of the sanctuary off the platform. The youth pastor's office was in a windowless room off a dimly lit basement hallway. None of the offices were identified.

The front door was kept locked even during office hours. If someone pushed the door buzzer and the secretary was in—which was less than half the time and not on any particular schedule—she would come down from the bell tower and open the door. Otherwise a person seeking help might never get in, even if the pastors were there.

As extreme as this actual example may seem, it is not all that rare. Even if a church doesn't make *all* these mistakes, offices that are unwelcoming, are inefficient, and cripple teamwork are amazingly common. Many church offices are cobbled together with little or no thought about what offices are supposed to do.

Because an effective staff team is at the heart of an effective church, one of the most strategic facility moves you can make is to give your (paid and unpaid) staff office space that enhances their effectiveness. When a church fails to do this, it ties the staff's hands, wasting staff time and money.

Great church offices do three things: welcome people, maximize efficiency, and promote team building.

Great Offices Are Welcoming

When we welcome guests into our homes, we greet them at the door, on the porch, or in the yard. We invite them in, take their coats and hang them up, and offer them our most comfortable seating. We offer them refreshments, tell them where the toilet facilities are, and do whatever else we can to make them feel at home.

If we truly want people to feel welcome in our churches, we will be no less intentional about welcoming guests to our church during the week. But anyone who tries to practice this kind of hospitality in a church office is likely to discover that the building was not designed with hospitality in mind. Most churches offer guests little more than a few chairs in the secretarial workspace.

When weekday guests enter the parking lot, they should be welcomed by an easy-to-find office entrance, preferably marked with a canopy, with guest and handicap parking located next to the entrance. If the office entrance is not visible from the street, clear signage should point the way. At the office entrance, office hours should be clearly posted.

Ideally the reception area should be just inside the exterior office entrance, so guests see the receptionist as soon as they enter the building. Guests are welcomed in a parlor-style waiting area where they can get information, rest, read, or visit, with refreshments available. Outside of office hours, this parlor can serve as a meeting room if the design carefully considers traffic patterns. Of course, for welcoming guests, a warm, friendly receptionist is most important of all.

This layout enhances security by allowing the receptionist to monitor who is coming and going. Sometimes a large window, glass door, or partial glass wall can open up a line of sight between the receptionist and the outside office entrance. If it is not practical to put the reception office just inside the entrance, signs should direct guests to the office.

The receptionist should serve as a gatekeeper for equipping staff. Office guests should not have direct access to the offices of pastors or other equipping staff without first checking in at—or passing through—the reception office. This is least important in small churches. But once a church reaches two hundred in average attendance, failure to do this causes problems. By the time a church reaches 350, this reception function becomes critical. Obviously, for the receptionist to be able to do this, all equipping staff must have offices in the same area.

In some churches, a foyer doubles as the reception office and waiting area during office hours. Lockable office furniture, perhaps an armoire that is attractive and yet can protect the computer and office records from the curious, may be helpful. Some churches have a reception counter in the foyer that doubles as a welcome center for worship services.

Great Offices Are Efficient

Whenever Christina printed from her computer, she had to make a trip to the other end of the building—almost a half-block away—to get her document from the printer.

Pastor Doug seldom delegated work to his assistant, whose office was in a different part of the building. He spent about ten hours a week doing work that could have been better handled by his assistant.

When Valerie was printing the Sunday bulletin, she found it almost impossible to take phone calls because the noisy copier was just a few feet from her desk.

While staff members may find these inconveniences frustrating, rarely do church leaders recognize how costly they are. If a church is spending $200,000 a year on salaries and benefits, and staff efficiency is 10 percent less than it should be due to poor office layout, the church is wasting $20,000 a year of its staffing budget.

Reconfiguring offices can be one of the simplest ways to eliminate waste from a church's budget and empower the staff to do its ministry.

One of the most common inefficiencies in small churches is that the secretary/reception office doubles as the workroom. When volunteers use the copier or other office equipment, they work in the reception office, interrupting the secretary's work. The secretary cannot even talk on the phone because the copier or folding machine is too noisy.

> **Reconfiguring offices can be one of the simplest ways to eliminate waste from a church's budget and empower the staff to do its ministry.**

The first step, therefore, to creating an efficient workspace is to create a central workroom. This room should include generous cabinet storage for office supplies, countertop workspace, and office equipment. This is often a great location for a computer workstation for volunteers. If possible, the reception office and all other support staff offices should cluster around a central shared workroom.

When asked if they prefer private or shared workspace, most office support staff tell us they prefer shared space. However, financial secretaries need privacy so confidential giving records are not seen by wandering eyes, and some administrative assistants who do computer work that is best done without interruption prefer private workspace. If in doubt about what kind of space will best serve your office staff, ask them.

Great Offices Promote Collaboration

Studies have shown that one factor more than any other predicts how closely coworkers relate to one another: proximity. It's not how close two people are on the organization chart; it's how close their workspaces are.

A great office brings the staff team together physically. It puts administrative assistants next to the equipping staff members they support. And perhaps the single most important space in the whole office complex is a commons area that is the hub of office activity. This is a break/lunchroom with a coffeepot, microwave, mini-fridge, and round table. This room should be at the center of the traffic flow of the office, a magnet that draws every staff member. It will spark much spontaneous heart-sharing and brainstorming. Many of your best ministry ideas will be born not in a regular meeting but in impromptu conversations over coffee in the break room. In some cases, the workroom and break room may be different ends of the same room.

This space changes behavior. Staff members spend more unscheduled time together. They share life more deeply. They share more ideas. While having a break room doesn't guarantee a healthy staff team, it is one of the most simple, practical, and powerful steps a church can take to grow a team culture within the staff.

> **Offices scattered throughout the building undermine teamwork, no matter how committed staff members say they are to being a team.**

Offices scattered throughout the building undermine teamwork, no matter how committed staff members say they are to being a team. If the youth pastor's office is in the youth building, away from the other staff offices, it almost guarantees that youth ministry will not be truly integrated into the daily life of the church but will function in its own silo. If the youth pastor needs a room in the youth building where he or she can hang out with teens during youth activities, provide it, but the primary youth ministry office should be with the rest of the staff. The same applies, of course, to worship and children's ministry staff. If the worship leader needs a work space in the choir room, that's fine, but if he or she works during office hours, the worship leader's office needs to be with the rest of the team.

Administrative assistants and the equipping staff members they serve need to work next to each other. If a pastor is at one end of the building and his assistant is at the other end, chances are close to zero that they are working effectively as a team.

A Few Tips

In addition to getting these "big three" right, attending to a few other details will help you create an office space that enhances ministry.

- Include a *conference room* for staff and ministry team meetings in or right next to the office area. This can double as a classroom.

- Many pastors have a small *conference table* in their offices for meeting with one to three people.

- Any office used for *counseling* should be soundproofed and have a window in the door. Some pastoral counselors have a direct exit from their offices so distraught counselees don't have to leave through the reception area. Churches with professional counselors on staff often have a separate counseling entrance for greater privacy.

- A *children's ministry workroom* in the children's area equipped with a copier and both office and craft supplies is a great way to resource your children's ministry workers and relieve congestion in the office workroom.

- In larger churches, it is helpful for the office of the *facility manager* (who oversees all the facility staff) to be with those of the staff team.

- *Office storage* is a key to efficiency. This starts with a generous workroom. A children's ministry workroom with plenty of storage for supplies is strategic. Make sure your music room has plenty of storage for music and (if applicable) choir robes. Musical instruments and staging are best stored next to the stage. Don't store old records in prime office space; attics and garages make great archive storage. Define who is responsible for keeping each storage area organized. Regularly cleaning closets can double your available storage space.

- *Plan for growth.* If you build just enough offices for your present staff team, as soon as your team grows you have a problem. When designing an office suite, consider building twice as much square footage as you need and use half the space for other ministries until you need more offices. Or design your offices so you can easily add on to them later.

- *Consider converting a residence.* If your church has offices scattered throughout your building or you just need more office space, look next door. While not all jurisdictions permit this, most homes can be easily adapted to church offices. If the church owns a parsonage next door to the church, giving the pastor a housing allowance and converting the parsonage to offices is often a great solution.

Creating great office space isn't about giving employees perks; it's about three big things: welcoming people, increasing efficiency (quit wasting staff dollars), and building teamwork that multiplies effectiveness. It's about empowering your staff to more effectively lead the church in carrying out its mission. Far more often than most people would imagine, creating a great office space is the most strategic facility investment a church can make.

Is Your Church Open for Business?

Find out how welcoming your church is to weekday guests by answering each question *yes* or *no*.

_____ 1. Does the appearance of your building and grounds welcome visitors?

_____ 2. Is there obvious, well-signed guest parking near the entrances?

_____ 3. Are the main entrances to the ministry center and offices visible and well-signed?

_____ 4. Are there canopies at these entries, extending to curbside, for unloading?

_____ 5. Is there a welcome sign with office hours and web address?

_____ 6. Will weekday visitors see the office entrance when entering the site? If not, are there signs directing them to it?

_____ 7. Are there windows at the entrances so people can be seen from outside?

_____ 8. Is there someone who greets people immediately at the office entrance?

_____ 9. Is there a comfortable, welcoming reception area at the office entry?

If you answered all ten questions *yes*, your church facility creates a warmly welcoming environment for weekday visitors. Each *no* presents an opportunity to make improvements to make your guests feel even more welcome.

21

One Church, Multiple Locations

Throughout the 1960s and 1970s, when a church ran out of seating in its Sunday worship service, the solution was to build. If the church couldn't afford to build, it either quit growing or took on heavy debt, limiting its ability to fund its ministries.

By the 1980s, innovative churches were adding a second service rather than building, and by the 1990s, multiple services were common. Many churches were holding three or more services as well as multiple sessions of Sunday school. These more-with-less building strategies allowed churches to grow faster and larger than before because they didn't have to pay huge sums for new buildings to make room for each wave of growth. They also allowed churches to direct more of their money to doing ministry rather than paying for buildings.

Around the turn of the century, another more-with-less building strategy began to gain traction—the multisite church. In 2000, there were still fewer than two hundred multisite churches (churches with multiple campuses) in the United States. By 2012, there were more than five thousand. Multisite churches, on average, reach and baptize more people than single-site churches, reach a greater diversity of neighborhoods, and activate a higher percentage of their people into ministry.[1]

Along with the multisite movement has been the move to multiple worship venues on the same campus. While the earliest form of multiple venues often involved having a traditional service in the sanctuary and a contemporary service in the gym, in time churches discovered that they could conduct two or more services simultaneously in multiple venues on the same campus. This was not the old concept of "overflow" seating. Rather, each venue was designed to be the preferred worship venue for those who attended.

In most cases, each venue had its own music team, allowing each venue to offer a different style of worship music. Each venue was designed to have its own feel—traditional, café, edgy, and so forth. Usually the preaching was live in the main venue, and by video in other venues.

Many large, growing churches combine the more-with-less building strategies of multiples services, multiple sites, and multiple venues. For example, North Coast Church, a pioneer in the multivenue/multisite movement, has four campuses in the San Diego area. Their main campus offers nineteen worship services, with twelve worship styles at six different times.

Their creative use of space allows North Coast to keep adding new services, new venues, and new campuses without borrowing. Prior to the launch of their newest campus, their website said: "We already have the money for the new campus in hand. We want to assure that, as always, we don't spend money we don't have or fall into the trap of 'if we build it, they will come.'"[2]

It is exciting to visit a church like North Coast to experience their creative worship and glean ideas. But if your church is small or medium, do multivenue or multisite worship have anything to offer you? More than you might think. Let's look at how multivenue and multisite strategies removed barriers to growth, first for a rural church of 145 and then for a suburban church of 670.

Zion Church

Zion was a traditional church meeting in a traditional country church building in the middle of a wheat field outside Abilene,

Kansas. Attendance had leveled off at 145 because that was all the sanctuary would hold.

The young pastor had a vision for reaching unchurched people. With the board's support, the pastor and a team of leaders started a Saturday evening service they called "a church within a church." It met in the fellowship hall and had a more casual feel to it than the Sunday worship service. Within a few months, it was averaging almost one hundred in attendance.

Still, since the Saturday service was attracting new people, it was not freeing up any space on Sundays to allow the Sunday service to grow. The solution the church came up with was to turn the fellowship hall into a video venue on Sunday mornings. Zion had two services at the same time on Sunday. Those in the sanctuary continued to have their traditional worship service and the group in the fellowship hall had a praise band and watched the sermon by video. By using their space more creatively, over a period of about two years attendance increased from 145 people at one service to attendance of between 250 and 300 at three services.

The pastor had a vision of moving the Saturday night service, called LifeHouse, into town where it would be easier to reach more people. Several of the leaders attended a multisite conference to explore the possibility of making Zion a multisite church. After months of consideration, the church decided not to become a multisite church but rather to launch LifeHouse as a church plant. Because Zion wanted to maintain its traditional DNA and LifeHouse was targeting a younger population that had little church background, they determined that the DNA of the two churches would be different enough that it would be more strategic for them to be governed separately. The pastor went with the new church plant and Zion hired a new pastor. Within a couple of years LifeHouse was thriving, averaging 250 in attendance and growing.

Multivenue/Multisite at Riverside

Skipp: In 2006, when we were out of space in two services and saw no way to increase our worship seating without taking on crippling debt, the video venue gave us a way out of our dilemma. By opening up a second venue for both services, we could keep growing without having to build right away.

The room we decided to convert to our video café was our fellowship hall. There were pros and cons to choosing this room. Because it adjoined our worship center, people did not feel physically separated from one another. They felt connected because they knew they were only a doorway apart. The downside was that because there was only a six-inch wall separating the two worship venues, sound traveled easily between the rooms, making it impractical for us to have a live worship band in the video café. As we talked with other churches that were using multiple venues, they all told us, "You have to have live worship!" For us, though, that wasn't an option. We had to do what worked for us.

We were also concerned about losing our "fellowship hall," but the exact opposite has happened. Our video café has become a great venue where fellowship takes place among all ages for all kinds of events several times a week—high school ministry, breakfasts for our seniors, weddings, funerals, and all kinds of gatherings.

When we decided to create our video café we didn't have any video equipment so we purchased a low-cost system—one live camera, two robotic camera/controllers, a basic switcher, and three projectors. We table-mounted the projectors and with special screen paint we created three screens on the wall. We framed the screens in 1 x 4s wrapped in black fabric. We built a basic portable audio system and used chairs we already owned to create seating for a hundred people.

We were surprised by people's reactions to our new venue. Many people comment that this room is probably a place for younger families and youth. I laugh and say people of all ages love this room. Many of our senior adults prefer our video café because they have a place to sit with their friends around a table, set their coffee down, and rest their Bibles and take notes.

Many people, including older adults, comment that the room feels more personal than the main auditorium. The two outside screens show a close-up of our teaching pastors, while the center screen shows a wide shot of the main venue platform. Because of the ratio of the screen size to the depth of the room, the speaker feels closer and the passion of the teacher is communicated better.

Because we are in Minnesota, you can count on at least one Saturday-Sunday blizzard every year. On these Sundays, our first service attendance is sparse. Shortly after we opened the video café we had one of these winter storms. Only seventy people showed up for our first service. Since our main venue seated five hundred, we expected everyone to sit there, but we actually had forty people in the main auditorium and thirty in the video café. People like different things!

Two years after creating our video café we made some upgrades. We bought a new switcher and an additional center screen robotic camera. We ceiling-mounted the projectors and installed a permanent audio system. We built an elevated second level in the back half of the room, two steps higher than the main floor, to create interest and better sight levels for viewing. We bought café tables and chairs of various heights, creating seating for an additional seventy people. The café seats are the first to fill as people enter the room.

The video café allowed us to go another six years before needing to add a third service. With our limited staff resources, this has enabled our church to continue to grow without overtaxing our leaders and volunteers. Now with three services on Sundays in two worship venues, we have begun using our gym as a third worship venue on high-attendance weekends such as Easter and Mother's Day. In this third venue we have a 12 x 12 video screen with live overlay of lyrics and teaching notes, and a quality portable sound system.

Today we are upgrading our video equipment once again to make our image formats comparable to what people are experiencing in their homes. This is preparing us to launch a second campus and also create programming for our local community on-demand fiber network system.

We are so thankful we didn't choose to go multisite before first creating multiple venues. This was an extremely low-risk, cost-effective facility solution. It also maximized our morning teams, while adding a second site would have required adding more staff and more teams of volunteers. The video venues have also allowed us to train a great team of volunteers with video skills so that they are now ready for the technical demands of doing multisite church. Being a multivenue church for several years has also helped our congregation and all of our volunteer teams understand what the next step to multisite will look like.

Explore the Possibilities

This chapter just scratches the surface of the possibilities and challenges of worshiping in multiple venues and at multiple campuses. There are excellent books, conferences, and consultants who can help you to learn from other churches' experiences as you launch additional worship venues or additional worship sites. Yes, it does require an investment in equipment and a commitment to learning new ways of doing church, but it opens the door for your church to reach far more people with the gospel at a fraction of the cost when compared to traditional facility solutions.

THE UTILIZATION TEST:
Do You Need to Build?

Which of the following statements are true for your church? Answer *yes, no,* or *n/a* ("not applicable").

_____ 1. Big groups are in big rooms. Little groups are in little rooms.

_____ 2. Our teaching methods maximize the use of space.

_____ 3. All unused or underused rooms have been identified and put to full use.

_____ 4. No rooms suitable for meeting are being used for storage.

_____ 5. Most furniture is moveable and can be arranged for maximum use of space.

_____ 6. Classroom tables are lightweight, folding, adjustable in height, and easy to move and store.

_____ 7. Worship chairs are comfortable, stackable, and easy to move and store.

_____ 8. Wherever possible, every space has been made multiuse.

_____ 9. We have at least three worship services.

_____ 10. We have multiple sessions of Christian education.

_____ 11. Some ministries are effectively conducted off-campus for less cost.

_____ 12. Homes are used for small groups and other ministries.

_____ 13. Community meeting rooms, restaurants, schools, etc., are used as needed.

We have researched the feasibility of the following:

_____ 14. Buying adjacent houses or buildings for church use.

_____ 15. Holding a simultaneous service in one or more video venues on our campus.

_____ 16. Adding another worship site.

Each *yes* answer identifies a more-with-less solution you are already implementing. Each *no* answer points to another opportunity to do more with less. Some may involve some inconvenience for the sake of the work of the church. All of these solutions have been successfully used as alternatives to building programs and relocation.

22

When It's Time to Build

How can you know when it is time to build? Ask your leaders to fill out the three tests in this book:

- The Motivation Test (p. 141) answers the question, "Are we building for the right reasons?"
- The Utilization Test (p. 187) answers the question, "Are there creative ways to meet our space needs without a major building program?"
- The Money Test (p. 226) answers the question, "Are we financially ready to build?"

Now answer one more question: "How healthy is our church?" Launching a major building program when the church is unhealthy invites disaster. The Natural Church Development survey (see ch. 3, n. 3) is probably the most widely used church health survey and is excellent. It can be a powerful tool not just to measure church health but to help develop a tailor-made action plan for strengthening your church's health.

Once you have passed the Motivation Test, the Utilization Test, and the Money Test, and determined that your church is healthy, only then are you ready to plan your building. If you have doubts about your readiness in any of these areas, resolve the problems before moving forward.

It is critical to keep the people of the church informed through each step of the planning. Start by presenting the answers to all the above questions along with the results of your church health survey. Take time to answer questions to earn the people's confidence that your leaders can be trusted with this responsibility. Invite members to submit ideas and comments in writing during the planning process.

Who Should Plan Your Building?

The experts, of course.

Ray: One church's building committee was made up of a cabinetmaker, a plumber, an electrician, a carpenter, and a residential interior designer. The pastor, who had no experience with building, was delighted to have these experts to make the decisions. The church ended up with fine cabinets, excellent plumbing and electrical systems, good carpentry, and an unusual color scheme. Most planning decisions were left up to me as the architect, with some input from the staff. I tried to make the best decisions without guidance from the church, but it was hard. Depending on the architect to make decisions that should have been detailed in the Program of Needs (see appendix A) is not the best approach. It happened often, however, during my years of practice.

> Planning and construction require different skills. Construction experts should serve during the construction phase; ministry leaders should decide what kind of space is needed.

Is it a mistake to rely on construction experts when the church builds? No, their skills are needed. The problem arises when they are expected to make decisions outside their areas of expertise. The key to avoiding this common mistake is to recognize that planning and construction are different functions that require different skills. Construction experts should serve during the construction phase; ministry leaders should decide what kind of space is needed for their ministries.

Planning for the Future

In place of the traditional building committee, we recommend that the church form a long-range planning team to guide the planning, and then a church health team and facility task force to implement the plans.

Long-Range Planning Team

Since the scope of the long-range planning team (LRPT) includes the total life of the church, the team should consist of people active in ministry and who, as a group, understand all major aspects of the church's life. This team's assignment is to conduct an in-depth assessment of the church's ministries, staffing, facilities, and finances, and then identify strengths and barriers to growth in each of these areas. Drawing on this assessment, the team will develop an integrated plan for removing these barriers, which includes prioritizing and sequencing action steps. Which needs to happen first to remove the next barrier to growth—hiring the next staff member or building an addition? Reconfiguring the offices or enlarging the foyer? Expanding the daycare center or expanding the youth ministry?

A major responsibility of this team is to write a Program of Needs for your facilities, a document that itemizes the facility needs for all the functions of your church. The team should consult with staff and leaders involved in administration, worship, children's ministry, student ministry, small groups, recreation, and outreach—every aspect of the church's ministry. If your church health team has already been formed at this stage, they can play a major role in identifying and prioritizing space needs for ministries.

Many churches enlist the help of outside professionals to conduct this in-depth assessment of the church's life and assist in developing the integrated plan. Normally, the LRPT determines if outside assistance is needed and, if so, researches and interviews consultants and recommends which group they believe can best meet the church's planning needs.

When the LRPT is exploring the feasibility of a major building program, their responsibilities include developing a preliminary project budget based on the Program of Needs they have written. For most projects, a professional estimator, building contractor, or architect must prepare this budget to ensure accuracy. Use this initial estimate to determine if the scope of the project is realistic for your people, following the guidelines in the next chapter. Appendix B shows how to prepare this budget and make design changes to reduce cost as needed.

Church Health Team

Once the LRPT has written its integrated plan, the church health team (CHT) is charged with taking the ministry (and sometimes staffing) recommendations and translating them into action. Drawing on the church health survey results and the recommendations of the LRPT, this team identifies three to five specific action steps that can be implemented or at least launched in the next twelve months. For each action step, they name what needs to be done, what person or group could best do it, and when it should be done. As action steps are completed, the team identifies additional action steps to improve the church's health. This team helps the church maintain momentum by limiting the number of action items, focusing on a short time-horizon, and adding next steps as action items are completed.

This group is advisory, not legislative, but if the team has the right members, their advice will carry such weight that almost all their recommendations will be accepted. They can make recommendations to a staff member, the board, a ministry team, or a committee. They can make very specific proposals, such as the creation of a new ministry team, including a suggestion as to who should lead it. Once the CHT has recommended an action step, a member of the team can be assigned to monitor the progress in implementing the assigned action step.

Because this group's mission is to strategize and prioritize, not directly implement, the team should consist of strategic thinkers, not necessarily detailed implementers. The team should include a member of the ministry staff, a member of the governing board, and a member of the LRPT. Six to eight team members is ideal.[1]

Facility Task Force

The facility task force (FTF) directs the implementation of the facility plan before and during construction. Their primary responsibility is to protect ministry leaders, paid and unpaid, from neglecting their ministry responsibilities or burning out during the building program. (See the guidelines in chapter 14 under "Losing Focus through Staff Burnout.")

The FTF responsibilities include:

1. Collaborate with the LRPT to select the architect.
2. Negotiate and approve the contract for architectural services. (All contracts should be approved by the church's attorney.)
3. Work with the LRPT to ensure the plans satisfy the requirements of the Program of Needs before they are approved for construction.
4. Oversee the bidding of contractors for construction or the selection of a building contractor.
5. Approve the construction contract and related items.
6. Monitor construction and approve payments.
7. Review and approve change orders, making sure any change is within the budget.

8. Keep the church's governing body informed during construction.

9. Approve completion and final payment.

10. Do the necessary follow-up during the year following completion.

If you do not have within your congregation people with the expertise to do all this, you may need to engage consultants during both the planning and construction phases.

Selecting Your Architect

Ray: I remember the pastor's panic: "The bids to build our new building are so high there is no way we can afford to build. We can't raise or borrow that much money, even if we could afford the debt payments." When I met with their finance board and building committee, I learned how this disaster had come about.

This church in Twin Falls, Idaho, had hired an architect who designed award-winning buildings for wealthy clients, mostly in the Sun Valley resort area of Idaho. The design had superb aesthetics, but the architect had not given them an estimate of the cost when they approved the preliminary or the construction documents. They didn't know the cost until they got the contractor's bid.

The architect's fee was substantial, based on a percentage of the bid. They had to put the plans in the "round file," as there was no way to modify them to lower the cost. It was an expensive education. I worked with them to develop utilization plans for their building that would allow them to almost double their attendance. They paid the architect, put their mistake behind them, and moved on with the real work of the church.

Finding out how an architectural firm operates is basic to making a wise selection. If the firm operates like the one in this story, they will design what they think you need with little input from you. The "right design" is everything; paying for it becomes your problem. Most churches cannot afford this approach as it requires an almost unlimited budget.

Some firms will serve you to the best of their ability, but have little or no cost-control during design and preparation of the construction documents, so the construction cost may come as a surprise. Other firms will tell you, "Our job is to design your project; the contractor will determine the cost." Cost-control is not part of the architect's education and may not be part of their professional practice.

My goal as an architect was to design the project to meet the need within the client's budget. Our contract stated, "If the bids to construct the project are higher than the approved budget, all necessary revisions to bring the work within the budget will be made at no additional cost to the client." The changes required to accomplish this did not include "a cheap building."

When you interview an architect, ask: (1) Will you include the above guarantee in the contract? and (2) How will you control the cost? Their answers to these questions, especially the second one, will tell you a lot about how they operate. Conduct this interview in the architect's office and ask to meet the staff at their work stations. Ask if engineering is done in-house or by outside consultants. (About half the cost is controlled by the engineering.) If your project includes a large gathering space, ask how the acoustical and sound system design is done. What is the fee? If their answers to these questions and others inspire confidence, take the next step of looking at some of their buildings. Ask some of the architect's clients about their services and cost-control during planning and construction. Also ask, "As you are using the building, is it meeting your needs? Does it operate well and with reasonable economy? What would you change if you could?"

A smaller firm will usually be best for smaller projects. Look at the scope of work the firm has done to determine if your project matches their abilities.

Finally, have the architect read and discuss chapters 13 to 21 of this book and your Program of Needs. Compare them with at least one other firm. Then decide whether to employ them.

If the firm you employ has little or no experience in church design, they will need guidance in meeting the needs of a church.

A firm that has designed schools will have the expertise needed for most church functions. This book describes the functional areas of the church that, along with your Program of Needs, can serve as a design guide for your architect.

Of course, a firm with experience in church design brings valuable knowledge. Some church design firms, however, tend to copy previous plans that may not fit your church. Don't base your decision on how many churches the firm has designed, but on the quality of their service and design.

What about Design-Build Firms?

Some church design-build firms do excellent work, but if you are considering working with a design-build firm, additional due diligence is needed. The church gives up a critical check and balance when the architect controls the construction and approves payments to the contractor. In most of these firms this control is missing. Many design-build firms also rely on stock plans that may not meet your needs, especially if your church is growing. In considering a design-build firm, check its reputation carefully as described above for an architect. Don't make a decision based on their fee, but on the quality of the product.

When it is time to build, remember, "Any enterprise is built by wise planning, becomes strong through common sense, and profits wonderfully by keeping abreast of the facts" (Prov. 24:3–4 TLB).

Part 4

More-with-Less Finances

The Principle of Provision

A church should not live by the world's financial system, but should operate within the income God provides.

23

Your Church Can Be Debt-Free

Skipp: My first weekend on staff at Riverside was the weekend we opened our new family life center. The church financed this $1.3 million addition with a combination of cash and debt. Over the next few years, while we chipped away at the mortgage, we kept borrowing more for necessary remodeling.

We felt stuck. Without more space we would stop growing, but because we were in debt and had no building fund, we couldn't afford to build. Unable to find a solution on our own, we asked for help.

During our first consultation with Living Stones in 2005, our church faced up to a painful reality: not only were we running out of space, but our debt payments were making it impossible for us to staff for growth. If we kept paying debt at the same rate and just "kept up" with facility maintenance, we would never escape our debt cycle and would never be able to hire the staff we needed to move forward. To keep growing, we had to find a way to remove our facility barrier and our staffing barrier at the same time.

The Three Principles

Of course, there is nothing unusual about Riverside's dilemma. Many churches need more space but don't have the money to build. In that situation, most churches stay stuck. Either they get by without building or they take on more debt that burdens them for years to come.

Riverside got unstuck because its leaders wholeheartedly embraced the three principles of more-with-less building.

The Principle of Focus

Eddy: Church leaders who see the size or appearance of their building as a sign of success are unlikely to make the transition from a debt economy to a provision (cash) economy. They probably won't be interested in the smaller-scale, multipurpose buildings that a pay-as-you-go approach usually requires.

People who see building buildings as the work of the church will want to keep building as fast as they can. They may see bigger buildings as better than smaller buildings. They won't want to wait until they can pay cash to build.

Riverside's leaders truly put people first. They weren't pushing to build a bigger building for appearance's sake. Over lunch, one of Riverside's elders said to the Living Stones team, "I have just one question: Where will our new auditorium be and how much will it cost us?"

I responded, "We believe we have found a way that Riverside can more than double in attendance without building a new auditorium, and you should be able to pay cash for the remodeling and additions that will be needed to make this work if your people step up and give."

The elder replied, "Then I'm satisfied. I'll wait till tomorrow's presentation for the details." That total absence of an empire-building mentality was an essential key to Riverside's being able to move forward.

The Principle of Use

Few growing churches can get out and stay out of debt unless they first change how they use and design buildings. For a congregation to be willing to do this, it must see buildings not as ends in themselves and not as signs of success or importance but rather as tools for ministry. Any church where people truly come first will welcome any strategy that enables it to put less time, money, and energy into buildings, and more time, money, and energy into ministering to people.

> **Few growing churches can get out and stay out of debt unless they first change how they use and design buildings.**

Riverside wholeheartedly embraced this principle. Our team's recommendations to Riverside actually included a couple of modest additions to Riverside's building. Riverside's leaders applied the principle of use so effectively in their facility that they have been able to more than double their attendance without adding a single square foot to their facility. They have remodeled extensively, invested in facility upgrades for multivenue worship, and made many programming and schedule changes to maximize the use of their facility.

The Principle of Provision

Embracing the principles of focus and use opened the door to a new possibility—transitioning from a debt economy to a provision (cash) economy. Many churches are lured into taking on crushing debt by the notion that they should build and borrow "on faith," only for time to expose that "faith" to be presumption.

To remove staffing barriers to growth, Riverside needed to pay off its debt and redirect the 10 percent of its budget going to debt payments to staffing. To remove facility barriers to growth, the church needed to remodel and upgrade technology. Both needs were equally urgent.

So the church conducted a capital campaign that raised $1.4 million over three years. Forty cents of each dollar given was applied to the debt and sixty cents to the remodeling and technology upgrades. At the end of the three years, the church was debt-free, it had hired an executive pastor and additional support staff, and the remodel had been completed for cash. Average attendance had increased by almost 50 percent.

Even after the three-year campaign, the church identified the remodeling projects and technology upgrades that were needed to continue to make the facility a better ministry tool. People continued to give to the fund and the church made the improvements on a pay-as-you-go basis. Riverside's building has become a living organism that adapts to the ever-changing needs of its ministries.

What about Capital Campaigns?

Raising the funds for a major building project normally requires a capital campaign. Some churches raise funds themselves; others hire consultants to conduct the campaign. Three-year capital campaigns are common, and a rule of thumb (depending on several variables) is that with the help of professional consultants a church can, over a three year period, raise about one and a half times its usual annual giving. So, for example, a church whose annual giving is normally $500,000 might raise an additional $750,000 for building during a three-year campaign.

Capital campaigns have gotten a lot of churches into trouble. This isn't because there is anything wrong with raising funds, but because many fund-raisers encourage churches to take on massive debt, or at least fail to warn churches against the dangers of debt.

There are times when a church's facility needs are so urgent that a push to raise a large sum of money quickly is needed. However, rather than spending as much as possible on building by borrowing as much as possible, you can make it the purpose of your capital campaign to pay off any existing debt and pay cash or almost cash for your building project. If your fund-raising consultants enthusiastically support this goal, they can be valuable allies in helping your church move from a debt economy to a provision economy.

Cash or Almost Cash

Skipp: Even a church that fully embraces the principles of focus, use, and provision may occasionally face a need so urgent that waiting to pay cash for the entire project would hinder ministry. To make room for the people God is sending us, Riverside will soon be opening a second campus. After that we may need to build a new facility on our main campus. We are considering conducting three one-year campaigns (so that in years two and three we include people who have just started attending). Depending on the final cost, we may or may not be able to pay cash for the full amount of these projects.

We are, though, passionately committed to paying cash or mostly cash as we expand, with the possibility of a modest short-term note if truly necessary to avoid hindering our growth. We are determined to never allow debt to interfere with our mission of reaching our community.

Your Church Can Do It Too

If the leaders of your church fully commit to the principles of focus, use, and provision, your church too can get out and stay out of debt, except for possible occasional short-term loans to meet urgent needs. Depending on your current debt load, deferred maintenance needs, and the urgency of your facility needs, it may take years, in some cases more than a decade, to reach this goal. Once you reach it, though, your church will be free to invest all your current income into present and future ministry, unleashing even greater potential for carrying out your mission in your community.

24

The Hidden Costs of Debt

What hidden costs and consequences does indebtedness pose, and what can churches do to minimize or avoid them?

In our credit-driven economy, the suggestion that even modest debt can limit freedom may sound like economic heresy. The credit card has become a symbol of freedom. We measure our financial strength by our credit rating and how much we can borrow.

The Bible describes a different relationship between freedom and debt. Proverbs 22:7 says, "The rich rule over the poor, and the borrower is slave to the lender" (NIV). In Israel, this slavery was literal. Debtors' prisons have been common through the centuries. The Bible does not say borrowing is a sin, but it does consistently present debt in a negative light. In Deuteronomy 28 a sign of God's blessing on Israel would be that they would lend and not borrow (v. 12); but if God cursed Israel, one evidence would be that they would borrow and not lend (v. 44).

Scripture can remove our cultural blinders and reveal debt's hidden costs. Then we can approach the decision to borrow or not to borrow with our eyes wide open to the actual costs.

Five "Hidden" Consequences of Church Debt

1. By presuming on the future, borrowing puts the church at unnecessary risk.

James writes, "Come now, you who say, 'Today or tomorrow we will go into such and such a town and spend a year there and trade and make a profit'—yet you do not know what tomorrow will bring. . . . As it is, you boast in your arrogance. All such boasting is evil" (4:13–16).

As the following true story illustrates, much borrowing is based on presumptuous assumptions.

Metro Church was planted as part of a rapidly growing suburban residential and business development. The church's growth to 2,500 in attendance and the growth of its campus paralleled the growth of both the community and the new denominational university next door to the church.

> **In our credit-driven economy, the suggestion that even modest debt can limit freedom may sound like economic heresy.**

Then during a five-year period the church built two major additions, taking on huge debt. As soon as the buildings were complete, growth almost stopped. As usually happens, the "build it and they will come" expectation was not realized. Giving remained strong and for a season the church was able to pay the mortgage. The seeds of decline, however, had been planted. Starting in 2006, "unforeseen" events triggered a decline of over eight hundred in attendance and more than two million dollars in annual giving.

- The church experienced a pastoral change, leaving the church without a key leader for a year.
- An economic recession began.
- The stock market crashed, adversely affecting the finances of many church members.
- The growth of the community stopped.

- University enrollment declined, forcing dismissal of faculty who were church members.

- A major donor's business went into bankruptcy. Many members' incomes declined.

- A prominent member and major contributor died.

- Decline created an environment that led to further decline. People abandon a sinking ship.

- The church had to reduce its ministry, staffing, and operating budget each year.

- The mortgage had to be refinanced for a longer repayment period.

- In an effort to reverse the decline, a new pastor introduced changes. Change, even positive change, is often experienced as loss. In response to the changes, people left the church.

- As of this writing, attendance and giving continue to decline.

This church's experience is typical of what happens when an indebted church runs into unexpected challenges. When the church operates in the world's economic system of debt, it is subject to the same dynamics that create global recession.

Operating debt-free, in contrast, prepares the church to weather an economic recession and other "unexpected" stresses. This church's story would have been far different if they had followed the biblical plan of provision to pay cash for new buildings after making maximum use of their existing buildings.

2. Borrowing tends to undermine contentment.

Paul wrote the Philippians that he had learned to be content with whatever he had, whether it was little or much (4:12–13). He wrote Timothy that "there is great gain in godliness combined with contentment" (1 Tim. 6:6 NRSV). Hebrews 13:5 exhorts us, "Keep your lives free from the love of money, and be content with what you have" (NRSV). In a culture where greed is considered normal, sometimes even virtuous, the biblical message of contentment is urgently needed and should be modeled by the church.

The main reason people borrow is because they are not content with living within their income. The church should call people to reject the always-wanting-more mentality of the world and to be content with God's provision. The most powerful way to teach this lifestyle is by example. What is right for the families of the church is right for the church. If the church preaches financial contentment but doesn't live it, its actions undermine its words.

3. Borrowing can desensitize us to people's needs.

When Paula was almost killed by an electrical shock in her home, the family immediately replaced the defective electrical panel responsible for the accident. Because they didn't have the seven hundred dollars needed for the repair, a member of their small group suggested that church families pitch in to pay for it. He felt that sharing within the body of Christ should ensure that no financial need within the body goes unmet (Acts 4:34). In the discussion that followed, someone said, "But lots of people make payments on things."

This church did end up generously helping the family, but in many similar situations churches have done nothing. When churches operate out of a debt-is-normal mindset, they are more likely to ignore the legitimate needs of their members caused by health emergencies, unemployment, accidents, or other crises, forcing their members to become slaves to debt.

When a church is committed to living within God's provision, emergencies that threaten to enslave fellow believers to debt are seen as opportunities to demonstrate caring and to protect one another's financial freedom through sharing.

4. Borrowing can deprive us of God's timing.

When God has directed us to pursue a particular ministry, we can confidently ask him to supply the resources to make it possible.

When God provides the money, we gratefully take God's provision as confirmation of his guidance to move ahead. But are we just as willing to accept God's withholding of funds as guidance? The greatest benefit of operating on provision rather than debt is that the lack of provision serves as a big caution flag. If God has not provided the funds, usually either the timing is wrong or the plan needs to be modified or abandoned. Borrowing can be a way of overriding this safeguard.

Faith acts in obedience to God's initiative. Presumption decides what to do and when, then asks God to bless it. Borrowing can be a way of getting around God's no, a way to move ahead on our own timetable rather than waiting on God's.

5. Borrowing can change the church's focus from people to money.

For many churches, this is the most damaging consequence of all.

Ray: A denominational superintendent in Africa who oversaw a large district of churches was faced with a serious decline in funds due to the worldwide economic downturn that started in many countries about 2006. When I asked him, "How did you survive the economic challenge?" he said, "We analyzed our needs and spending. Then we made changes that not only saved money but actually improved our operations! We knew these improvements were needed, but it took a recession to force us to make them."

"Did you have to deal with debt as you made these changes?" I asked.

"No," he said, "we operated without debt and that gave us the freedom to make creative changes." This is a great example of doing more with less.

When a church is debt-free, it has many more opportunities to do more with less than churches that are burdened by debt.

25

Getting off the Roller Coaster

When we help churches with facility planning, nine times out of ten the design concept we propose can be built debt-free. In the other cases, we recommend short-term borrowing as part of a long-term plan for the church to become debt-free.

While many church leaders are excited to learn how they can meet facility needs without debt, others see no reason to avoid borrowing. Many church board and building committee members work in businesses where debt is normal or even necessary. If it makes good business sense at the office, why not at the church?

> **Debt, used prudently, has many advantages for profit-making businesses. Almost none of the benefits of debt, however, apply to the church.**

Actually, that's a terrific question. Most businesses do operate with debt, and most use it responsibly. Debt, used prudently, has many advantages for profit-making businesses. Almost none of the benefits of debt, however, apply to the church.

What benefits do businesses receive from borrowing?

1. *Business property produces income.* Business owners borrow to buy and develop real estate because they expect the property to generate enough income to make the mortgage payments and generate a profit.

   Church buildings don't exist to produce income. The cost of church buildings is an expense, not a business investment.

2. *Business property usually appreciates.* Business owners may prefer to buy buildings, even with heavy indebtedness, rather than rent, because good quality buildings usually increase in value.

   Church buildings usually depreciate due to limited resale value.

3. *Business debt brings tax advantages.* For businesses, interest, depreciation (even when the actual market value of the property is increasing), and facility operating costs are all tax deductible. Profits from the sale of business property (capital gains) are often taxed at a lower rate than other income.

   Churches get no tax advantages from owning property.

4. *Businesses can use real estate equity as leverage to buy more property.*

   The church is not in the business of leveraging property to buy more property with the goal of making a profit.

5. *The option of bankruptcy allows a business to take on risk.* Risk is inherent when operating on debt, a normal aspect of doing business. If the business goes "sour," bankruptcy is available for reorganizing or canceling contractual commitments.

   If a church is forced into bankruptcy, it is still morally responsible to repay all debts.

While debt has both benefits and risks for the business owner, when a church borrows it takes on all the risks of debt without enjoying any of these benefits. For all of these reasons we advocate the Principle of Provision: *A church should not live by the world's financial system, but should operate within the income God provides.*

The World's Financial Roller Coaster

Financial history is a roller-coaster ride of profits on the way up and losses on the way down. While there will always be natural ups and downs, a debt-based economy exaggerates the "ups," creating bubbles, and when those bubbles burst, what might have been a mild downturn can become a crash.

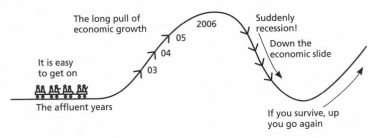

When a church operates on debt, it enjoys few of the benefits of the "up" cycles, but suffers all the consequences of "down" cycles. When the church shifts from a debt economy to living within God's provision, God's work is protected from most, if not all, of the crippling effects of recession. It is able to adjust to the changing economy and continue ministering to the needs of people both inside and outside the church, especially those who have extra needs during an economic storm.

A Time to Borrow?

Given all the downsides of church debt, is there ever a time to borrow? We believe there are a few narrowly defined situations when borrowing may be wise or necessary.

1. When rent is exorbitant, borrowing may be better.

When the cost of buying or building—including mortgage payments, insurance, maintenance, repairs, utilities, and so forth—is less than the cost of renting, borrowing may be cost-effective.

2. Borrowing to buy adjacent property for expansion can be wise.

If the church needs more land, the time to buy adjacent property is when it comes on the market. If there is a building on the property, you may be able to use it for classes, offices, a nursery, students, or staff housing for far less cost than a new building. Check with your zoning department about the requirements to use the property for church purposes. If you have no immediate need for the space, you may be able to rent it temporarily.

Borrowing to buy rental property is wise only if the purchase meets the following conditions.

- *Rental income covers most or all expenses*, including mortgage payments, maintenance, insurance, and other operating expenses.

- *The property stands alone as collateral* with an exculpatory clause in the mortgage agreement. Consult your real estate agent and attorney for advice.

- *The resale value of the property exceeds the loan amount*. If the church cannot make the payments, it can sell the property and pay off the note.

- *The note can be paid off by the time the church needs to use the property*. If the church expects to need the property in five years, take out a five-year note so the church will pay off the mortgage by the time the rental income stops.

- *No money is taken from ministry to pay for the property*. The church should buy the property only if it can make the down payment and set aside a reserve fund to cover periods of vacancy and emergency repairs without taking money from ministries.

- *People other than pastoral staff are able and willing to manage the rental property*. Managing rental property can be a time-consuming job involving lots of hassles. Pastoral staff should never have to take time from pastoring to manage church-owned rental property.

When the church buys and manages rental property by these guidelines, no funds are diverted from the ministries of the church and the rental income helps provide for future expansion.

3. Churches sometimes must borrow during their transition from a debt economy to a provision economy.

Once a church commits to becoming debt-free, it may take several years for it first to pay off its mortgage and then to build up a provision fund for the next building project. A commitment to operate by provision is usually accompanied by a strong focus on ministry, which results in growth, requiring full utilization of existing facilities, remodeling, and additions.

If a growing church has exhausted all other more-with-less building solutions and cannot increase capacity without borrowing, short-term debt may be necessary. To refuse to borrow in this situation could cripple the church's growth. Nine out of ten churches, though, have creative options available that do not require borrowing.

4. Loss of the building due to natural disaster or other circumstances may make borrowing unavoidable.

A plan for housing the congregation should be accompanied by a financial plan for becoming debt-free. Creative meeting-space solutions can often make borrowing unnecessary.

When a church borrows for any of these reasons, the short-term debt should be structured as an interim step in a long-term plan to become and stay debt-free. When the church takes strict precautions, it limits the downside risks of the debt roller coaster and hastens the day when the church will enjoy total freedom from debt.

No More Building Funds

Ray: When I was a practicing architect I never could have imagined saying this, but I no longer believe in church building funds. It's not that I don't believe a church should save for future facility needs; I urge churches to save the entire amount needed before building so they can build debt-free. The money being saved, however, shouldn't go into a building fund; it should go into a *provision fund*. A church in the San Francisco Bay area taught me why this is so important.

As the pastor of the church neared retirement, he wanted to leave behind a new church building as his crowning achievement, so he hired an architect to draw up plans for the building of his dreams. The design was flamboyant and impractical, but some people in the congregation supported the pastor's dream anyway and gave about $200,000 to the building fund. Though this is a good bit of money, it was not nearly enough to start the building. Then the pastor died of a heart attack.

A young, energetic pastor was called to the church and the church began to grow. They added a second service, creating the need for a fellowship foyer to handle the traffic between services. To provide more offices for the growing staff, the church needed to remodel to convert the parsonage into an administrative center.

The congregation knew the building the former pastor had designed didn't fit the church's needs and never would and that it would never be built. But when the pastor asked the building fund donors if they would release those funds so the church could remodel, they refused. The wife of the former pastor, still active in the church, along with several of her friends, remained intent on building the unnecessary building as a monument to the former pastor.

Because the building fund had $200,000, the rest of the congregation wasn't motivated to give money to pay for the urgently needed remodeling. The pastor tried for five years to break this impasse before finally giving up and resigning.

This tragedy could have been avoided if the church, rather than having a building fund, had started a provision fund. A church saves money for future facility needs in this fund, but with the understanding that the church can use it in whatever ways best serve the mission of the church as it grows. Rather than enlarging its building, the church might, for example, use these funds to launch a new campus or plant a new church. Or rather than building, the church might use money from this fund to hire a new staff member who would make it possible for them to add another service. A provision fund can be invested wherever it is most strategic for the continuing outreach and growth of the church, whether for facilities, staff, operations, or sharing.

Temple Bible Church in Temple, Texas, was a young, growing church meeting in rented space. They had purchased and paid for a property and raised most of the money needed to start building. Then a member of the church, a pilot, developed a brain tumor and needed surgery. He was between jobs and so had no health insurance. Without hesitation, the church decided to use whatever church funds were needed to pay for his surgery. The church truly needed a building, but this member's needs came first.

Word of what the church was doing got out and money started coming in to help with the surgery, even from other states. In the end, the donations received for the surgery replaced all the money taken from the building fund with $200 to spare. Though they didn't call it that, this church had a provision fund—a fund intended primarily to meet future facility needs, but available to meet any other needs that might take priority. This church put the needs of people first, and when they did, their need for facilities did not go unmet.

26

From Vision to Provision

One church struggling to meet its budget surveyed its members to find out why people weren't giving more. Here are some of their answers:

> "We pay our pastor, support the staff and programs of the church, take care of our church buildings, and give to missions. What else is there?"

> "I would give more, but there is no need since there is no outward mission. I would rather support the agencies that are doing things I believe in."

> "To me it is a question of priorities. Over 90 percent of the budget is for internal things. The budget reflects a lack of congregational vision. What are our goals?"

> "I would consider giving more if I knew how the money was being used and how more money would be used."

> "I didn't vote for borrowing to build and am tired of hearing about paying the debt. If we didn't have debt, there would be more money."

The low level of giving wasn't because people didn't want to give; it was because they wanted their giving to count.

The Dreaded Sermon

Why do so many people hate sermons on giving? Is it because they are selfish? They just don't like to give? We suspect the main problem lies elsewhere—with sermons that appeal mostly to duty.

While guilt can motivate giving in the short-term, it is a lousy long-term motivator. In fact, negative motivations for giving are not even biblical. As a part of his biggest fund-raising effort, Paul wrote, "Each of you must give as you have made up your mind, not reluctantly or under compulsion, for God loves a cheerful giver" (2 Cor. 9:7 NRSV). Paul was not above scolding, but we never see him scolding to motivate giving.

Cheerful, generous giving is inspired by passionate commitment to a vision. A call to sacrificial generosity needs to be tied to a vision of transforming people's lives.

From Debt to Provision

Academy Church in Colorado Springs was drowning in debt. To overcome the financial challenges as well as the people's discouragement, the leaders clearly defined a new vision for people to rally around. They adopted a three-year integrated plan with four components: a financial plan, a staffing plan, a facility plan, and a ministry plan.

The *financial plan* provided for regularly reporting to the congregation on giving and spending, changing spending priorities, and increasing giving to pay debt and expand ministry.

The *staffing plan* called for replacing staff that had been lost during the church's financial crisis. Strategically expanding the staff was essential to implementing the ministry plan.

The *facility plan* addressed deferred maintenance needs that had been neglected during the church's financial crisis. A facility utilization plan provided for accommodating growth to more than double its current attendance without a major building program.

The *ministry plan* was central to the integrated plan, since the ministry plan was the driver for the financial plan, the facility plan, and the staffing plan. Academy Church embraced the goal of activating the people into ministry with the motto, "Every Believer a Minister." The church offered classes to help people see how their spiritual gifts and personality traits equipped them for ministry. Apprenticeships, leadership training events, and small groups supported people as they took on new ministries. The primary focus of the staff shifted from doing ministry to equipping every member for ministry, with a new staff position devoted entirely to helping members succeed in their ministries.

The integrated plan was presented to the congregation then discussed in smaller groups in homes, with these conversations generating more ideas. The congregation responded enthusiastically with commitments to ministry and increased giving. Over the next three years the church accelerated its mortgage payments, caught up on deferred maintenance, and expanded staff. The enthusiasm was contagious and the church grew.

At the end of the three years the church updated its plan. The new financial plan included reduced mortgage payments to leave more money for other needs. The plans for ministry, staff, and facilities were updated for the next five years to reflect the higher attendance and giving.

After eight years, though the church was still not debt-free, it was well on its way. The entire journey to financial freedom took thirteen years, resulting in a healthy, growing church of over a thousand in attendance.

What made the difference? A vision that inspired the people to give generously of their time, money, and energy.

Giving to a Vision

Ray: When Pastor Brian Kelly of McLane Church called, it was for the usual reasons. Located in a rural area near Erie, Pennsylvania, the church had outgrown its facilities and didn't know what to do next. They had already added a second service. They were desperately short on parking. Their Sunday school classes were overflowing their space. For years this church had been debt-free and was committed to keeping it that way. How could they meet their space needs without going into debt and taking funds away from ministry?

As pressing as McLane's facility needs were, their most pressing need was for staff. Brian had become their pastor when the congregation had dwindled to fewer than forty people and the church's survival was uncertain. In the three years since, the church had grown to over two hundred but had not added an associate pastor. Brian was overwhelmed.

We outlined a remodeling plan that would give the church room to double without new construction. We reaffirmed the need for an associate pastor and a full-time secretary. There was, however, no money to meet these needs.

An analysis of their finances revealed that their sixty-four giving units were, on average, giving 4 percent of their income. For this church to take these next steps of growth would require a giving level of 6 percent. One of two things was going to happen: either giving would increase or growth would stop.

Even after immediate barriers to growth were removed, future needs for staffing, facilities, and local missions would require more giving. I proposed a five-year financial plan that called for increased giving of 1½ percent for each of the first two years, then an additional 1 percent for the next three years, raising the church's average giving level from 4% to 10%.

Evidently my proposal was too modest for the people of McLane. The congregation unanimously adopted a budget based on increasing giving not by 1½ percent but by 2 percent, effective immediately. They decided to hire another secretary immediately, add a full-time associate pastor in six months, and make facility improvements within nine months. After this vote Brian sent a short, low-key letter to the people of the church reporting the decision and asking each family to prayerfully consider increasing its giving by 2 percent of its income and to plan for future increases. Weekly giving immediately jumped and continued to increase long-term. Today this church is alive and well with weekly attendance of over a thousand.

Developing a Culture of Generosity

Skipp: As Riverside Church continued to get healthier, we were seeing consistent growth in all areas except finances. In 2008 I read a tweet from Anthony Coppedge. It said that churches need to change their prayers from, "God, please provide more volunteers, more resources, and so on," to "God, would you find us *trustworthy* as a church to handle more volunteers, more resources . . .?" God wants churches he can trust.

> **Every monetary gift is a spiritual step.**

As we reach more people in our community, we want to make sure we can help them become fully devoted followers of Christ. To do this we need systems that help people connect through serving, participating in small groups, and taking specific spiritual steps. We had some systems in place, but we knew we could be using them much more effectively.

One of the things we have learned through connecting with many churches around the country is that as your church develops more clearly defined processes for how you do things, your people will take more spiritual steps. We believe that every monetary gift is a spiritual step. We treat it that way when people give their time or talents, and we need to treat it that way when they give money as well.

A Funding Plan

As we learned through Giving Rocket, in most churches the leaders create a spending plan but few create a funding plan.[1] That had certainly been true at Riverside. We spent two years researching and experimenting with what we were learning. In 2012 we created our first annual funding plan using many tools from Giving Rocket.

- Our whole staff team handwrote thank-you notes to first-time givers.
- We sent first-time givers a small booklet called "What Happens When You Give."
- Every week one of our leaders gave a two- to five-minute "giving talk," sharing about how God had been at work and how the investment we were making was impacting people for Christ. We focused not on our needs, but on what God was doing and how we could be a part of it.
- We sent out a monthly email report (and snail mail to those without email) called "Your Giving Making a Difference," and posted it on our website.
- We started sending out giving statements every quarter, not just at the end of the year.
- We provided new ways to give and encouraged people to use them. There are many ways to give digitally—directly from the bank, with a mobile app, through a giving kiosk, or from our website. Most weeks 40 to 60 percent of our giving is now digital.

Lessons Learned

It took us a couple of years of research, trial, and error to develop an effective funding plan. Here are a few lessons we learned along the way.

1. *Research, research, research.* We don't need to re-create everything. A lot of work has already been done. We can take advantage of those resources. For example, we learned that new attenders take three to five years to develop a "tithing" level of giving. We didn't need to redo the research to learn this.
2. *Adapt what you learn to your church's culture.* Which systems fit our church? Which do not? How do we need to tweak resources and methods to make them work for us?

3. *Define what a culture of generosity looks like.* How will we measure generosity? How will we gather, track, and report this information? We decided to track first-time givers, total giving units, consistent givers, and "tithers"—households that give at a level of about one-tenth of our community's median income. We also track and celebrate the number of digital givers.

4. *Keep pointing to how generosity impacts ministry.* Paying off our debt was the main way we freed up funds to fully staff for greater effectiveness and growth.

5. *Treat stewardship as a spiritual discipline.* We decided to celebrate decisions to give as spiritual steps, just as we celebrate other spiritual steps.

6. *Involve every staff member and key leader in your funding plan.* It is not enough for ministry leaders to shape your spending plan; they need to take equal responsibility for the funding plan.

7. *Always keep the focus on the vision, not on the balance sheet.*

Only once before in our church's history had we met our budget goal for giving. The first year we fully implemented our funding plan, our giving exceeded our budget, and not just by a little—by 15 percent! This is exciting not because it improves our balance sheet, but because it increases our capacity to minister to people.

Cheerful Generosity

These three congregations faced financial challenges, each for different reasons. In each case, a compelling vision captured people's hearts and minds, and they gave generously not out of duty or obligation or guilt, but because it brought them joy to invest in something they passionately believed in.

─────────── **God on Giving** ───────────

by Peggy Heid

The Bible has many verses about giving. Here are a few of them.

1. **God sets the example.** "God so loved the world he *gave* . . ." He puts his generosity on display and says, "Follow me."
2. **God asks (actually commands) us to give.** This seems obvious, yet as church leaders we are often timid about asking. When God wanted to supply the needs of the departing Israelites, he instructed them to ask their neighbors for gifts (Exod. 11:2). Paul reminds Timothy of the importance of asking people to give (1 Tim. 6:17–19).
3. **God commands proportional giving.** Throughout the Old Testament, God instructs his people to give a percentage of what they have received. Paul instructed the Corinthians to give in proportion to their income (1 Cor. 16:2).

Proportional giving overcomes our tendency toward self-deception when evaluating our generosity. We might assume that wealthier people give away more of their income. Wrong! Among the churches we have worked with, we discovered that the wealthier the congregation, the *lower* the percentage of their income they gave to the Lord's work.[2] Lower-income congregations actually gave more generously. In churches where households earned less than $60,000, supporting households gave an average of 6.7 percent of their income to the ministry, but in churches where the average income was over $60,000, average church supporters only gave 4.8 percent to the church.

	Avg. Income Less Than $60,000	Avg. Income Greater Than $60,000
All Giving Units	4.3%	3.1%
Supporting Giving Units*	6.7%	4.8%

*Supporting Giving Units are households that contribute at least $500 per year to the church.

4. **Proportional giving requires ongoing evalua-tion.** Rather than calculating a figure and then setting the autopilot, giving requires occasional recalculation. In the Old Testament, the agrarian rhythms dictated an evaluation of the level of giving with each harvest and cycle of livestock. Paul suggested proportional giving take place weekly (1 Cor. 16:2).

God's approach to fund-raising reveals some practical implications for churches. First, church leaders must be living generous lifestyles before calling on their congregations to do so. Second, we need to trust in God's ways and not be afraid to ask. Third, since God asks people to give in terms of percentages, so should we. Charts like the one below can help parishioners convert their contribution dollars into percentages. Fourth, evaluating our giving needs to be part of an ongoing rhythm. Since generosity is so crucial to making disciples, churches may want to promote this self-examination every New Year or fall.

One strategy we recommend is to challenge members of the congregation to increase their giving by 1 percent. If done consecutively for two to three years, this can increase giving by hundreds of thousands of dollars even for a church of less than two hundred.

Figure 26.1

Would you consider taking the 1% challenge?

Locate your annual income and current monthly giving on the chart. Move to the right to grow in your monthly giving.

Annual Income	1%	2%	3%	4%	5%	6%	7%	8%	9%	10%	11%	12%	13%	14%	15%
$20,000	$17	$33	$50	$67	$83	$100	$117	$133	$150	$167	$183	$200	$217	$233	$250
$30,000	25	50	75	100	125	150	175	200	225	250	275	300	325	350	375
$40,000	33	67	100	133	167	200	233	267	300	333	367	400	433	467	500
$50,000	42	83	125	167	208	250	292	333	375	417	458	500	542	583	625
$60,000	50	100	150	200	250	300	350	400	450	500	550	600	650	700	750
$70,000	58	117	175	233	292	350	408	467	525	583	642	700	758	817	875
$80,000	67	133	200	267	333	400	467	533	600	667	733	800	867	933	1,000
$90,000	75	150	225	300	375	450	525	600	675	750	825	900	975	1,050	1,125
$100,000	83	167	250	333	417	500	583	667	750	833	917	1,000	1,083	1,167	1,250
$125,000	104	208	313	417	521	625	729	833	938	1,042	1,146	1,250	1,354	1,458	1,563
$150,000	125	250	375	500	625	750	875	1,000	1,125	1,250	1,375	1,500	1,625	1,750	1,875

The Money Test:
Are You Financially Ready to Buy or Build?

Which of the following are true for your church?

_____ 1. Our church is debt-free.

_____ 2. We consistently meet our budget, fully funding our ministry and staffing needs.

_____ 3. Our staffing budget reflects our commitment to staff for growth by hiring staff ahead of growth.

_____ 4. Our budget includes 1 to 2 percent for equipping unpaid ministry leaders and team members.

_____ 5. Our people have made pledges to increase giving to cover the cost of construction and future building operating costs so that none of the church's present ministry spending is diverted to building.

_____ 6. The increased giving for future facility needs has been invested in an interest-bearing provision fund.

_____ 7. The church now has enough in its provision fund to be able to pay cash or mostly cash for the proposed project.

If you checked statements 1 through 4, your church is basically financially healthy. By taking the steps described in statements 5 through 7, you should be financially ready to build within a few years. When all seven statements are true, you pass the financial readiness test.

Conclusion

The Blessing of Inconvenience

Skipp: More than doubling Riverside's attendance in a building that we thought was already full not only required creativity and a willingness to try new things, but time after time, it has meant choosing to be inconvenienced. We would love to have a bigger worship center, more connections space, more classroom space, and offices that aren't quite so cozy. It would be easier to offer fewer performances of our special productions instead of making room for everyone who wants to attend. It would be less stressful to not have to do so many services every weekend. Coming up with creative ways to meet the space needs of our growing ministries is a never-ending challenge. There are times we wish we could do more with more, rather than always having to do more with less.

But then we look at what God is doing. We see new people coming to Riverside. We see people saying yes to Christ. We see people's growing commitment through sharing life in small groups, serving, and giving. We see kids and students excited about their faith and inviting their friends. We see relationships being reconciled and marriages being healed. In all these areas the church is stronger and healthier today than in years past. By spending less on buildings and financing, we have had more resources to invest in ministries and staffing. By choosing to spend less on making church more convenient for us, we have seen thousands of lives changed for eternity.

We would love to have a more convenient building, but we would never trade the opportunities God has given us these past few years to reach more people than ever before for the conveniences of a bigger building. What a privilege!

ONLY GOD!

Acknowledgments

We want to thank the hundreds of churches that have invited the Living Stones team to walk alongside them during seasons of strategic planning. They have been our mentors. Almost everything in this book we have learned from them, from both their successes and their failures.

A big thanks to research assistant Kathy Roesler for many hours of compiling and analyzing financial data on churches Living Stones has worked with through the years. For reading the manuscript and offering many helpful suggestions, we thank Peggy Heid, Val Battis, and Joylin Hall.

Finally, we thank Chad Allen, editorial director at Baker Books, who invited us to submit a proposal for a book to update and replace *When Not to Build*. For more than two decades, Baker has been a wonderful publishing partner.

Appendix A

How to Write a Program of Needs

Your architect should not design in a vacuum. Without knowing the specific needs of your church, some architects will rely on traditional designs that do not meet the requirements of a growing congregation. The Program of Needs is a written document that itemizes the facility needs and desires for all the functions of your church. The long-range planning team does not design a building; it defines what it wants the building to do. It is the architect's job to design a building to meet all these needs. Even so, writing a Program of Needs is a demanding task and in many cases will require the help of a professional church facility consultant or architect who understands the special needs of growing churches.

Which of the features described below (and in other parts of the book) are desirable? Highlight each of the features you want to incorporate into your design. Give your architect a highlighted copy of the book and your written Program of Needs.

Ministry Center

At the heart of more-with-less church design is the multiuse ministry center, not a single-use worship space. What functions will take place in this space? Your answer to this question will determine your needs for equipment, movable versus fixed staging, lighting, acoustical treatment and sound system, and active storage adjacent to the room.

Central to the operation of the ministry center is the use of movable worship chairs for seating. Church chairs are stored by stacking, not folding. They are upholstered, more comfortable than pews, have wood or steel frames, and can be ganged together. They may cost more than pews but are worth it, because they increase your seating capacity and make the room usable for multiple ministries throughout the week. The flexibility to adjust the seating to the attendance solves the size problem.

If you are considering building a sanctinasium—a combination gym and worship center—as your ministry center, be aware of the following requirements for making it workable:

- A gym-type carpeted floor
- Acoustical treatment for speaking and music
- A sound system designed for this space, with a movable console
- A dual lighting system: high-intensity lighting for recreation and appropriate lighting that can be dimmed for worship and other uses, together with theatrical lighting and controls for the platform area
- Large active storage rooms for equipment and furniture
- Preparation rooms for drama and other productions
- Dressing rooms for recreation

The key to making a sanctinasium work is to design it primarily to satisfy the needs of worship and other services, including the gym functions, rather than to design a typical gym and then use it for worship.

Fellowship Foyer/Community Plaza

For the growing church we recommend a fellowship foyer or community plaza that combines the functions of the foyer and fellowship hall. This becomes one of the most intensely used multiuse spaces in the building. When a church goes to multiple services in a building designed for single services, the addition of a fellowship foyer may be essential to making multiple services practical. This is where people leaving one service connect with those arriving for the next one.

The location of the fellowship foyer or community plaza is critical. It is located between the worship center and the most-used entrances of the building so that all or most visitors pass through this area going to and from worship. For churches with multiple worship venues, it is ideal when a single fellowship foyer can serve all the worship venues as a way of connecting people who attend various services.

Ideally, a fellowship foyer is 50 to 60 percent of the square footage of your worship center. This space includes a welcome center, handicap-accessible restrooms, a serving kitchen, and active storage for the furnishings and equipment that will be used for meals and other activities held in this space. In large churches, this space is often even larger and is called a community plaza, including such features as a gourmet coffee bar, a section of café seating, furnishings to create conversation centers, and a bookstore. It may or may not be designed to be subdivided so that multiple activities can be held in this space simultaneously.

If desired, a moveable wall between the ministry center and foyer/plaza allows the two spaces to be used together when needed. In some cases, this space can be designed to accommodate additional seating, as a video café worship venue, or as future expansion space for the main worship center. It is often most practical to build a fellowship foyer as an addition to an existing building, though some churches can create this space through remodeling.

Glass doors and walls allow people outside to see people inside, inviting people in through what they can see. Outdoor terraces around the entrances to the foyer/plaza also invite people in and enlarge the functional area of the foyer/plaza in fair weather.

Classrooms

The kind of space needed for education varies with the age group. Modify the following recommendations to meet the needs of your church.

Nursery

If the church serves young families, careful planning of the nursery area should be a high priority. For many parents with nursery-age children, an excellent nursery and staff is the single most important factor in choosing a church home.

Ideally, the nursery check-in should be accessible from the fellowship foyer, located conveniently near the worship center but far enough away that worshipers are not distracted by the noise of children. Provide extra corridor space or alcoves at the entrances to the nursery rooms so parents can check in and pick up their children without entering the rooms or creating congestion.

Design separate spaces for toddlers, crawlers, and crib babies, with each room having a maximum capacity of twelve to fifteen children plus workers. In smaller churches, toddlers and babies can be in the same room with a gate-type divider keeping toddlers from stepping on younger babies, while still allowing two nursery workers to staff the whole room. If possible, provide a sleeping room just off the crib room that is completely visible to crib room workers. A room where mothers can care for and feed their children should have its own entrance.

Equip each room with individual cubicles for each child's personal items, including diaper bags, just inside the door. Each room should have an adult-size toilet, counter, and sink. Have a storage closet for toys, supplies, folding playpens, and other equipment in each room.

Provide a check-in system for each child. Know who is and is not authorized to pick up each child. Medium and large churches need an electronic paging system for notifying parents when they need to come to the nursery to care for their child.

Elementary-age children

While rows of small rooms work well for children's classes in small churches, medium and large churches need large, flexible spaces. A single-age group can grow to thirty or forty in one room if the adult-to-student ratio is appropriate. Movable sight breaks and storage units on wheels can be used to subdivide open spaces for age groupings. Each room is supervised by a lead teacher who is assisted by one worker for each four to five preschoolers, each five to six primaries, or each eight to ten older children. Workers serve as caregivers at tables or in activity groups and help to maintain control when the whole group is assembled. (See "The More We Teach Together" following chapter 19).

The design of this kind of classroom should include excellent sound absorption, a work counter with a sink and drinking fountain, and a toilet facility so children need not leave the room or area. A room for supplies and storage is needed. Medium and large churches need check-in counters and electronic paging systems for parents.

Teens

There appears to be no upper limit to the size of the junior high and senior high departments. The bigger the group, the better the teens seem to like it. Large churches that have tried to divide the teens (into two sessions of Sunday school, for example) have usually found it does not work; the teens all gravitate to one session. The best way to accommodate a growing teen ministry, therefore, seems to be to provide larger rooms as the teen group grows. This makes planning facilities for a growing youth group a challenge.

One solution is to use a movable sound-wall system. Another is to plan walls that can be removed for expansion into adjacent space. You can build and remove inexpensive gypsum walls several times before their cost will equal that of a sound-wall system. Or you can plan a variety of room sizes and move the group to ever-larger rooms as needed. Whichever solution you choose, it is critical to design the room for high decibel levels (what adults call noise).

Like other parts of the building, the teen meeting areas should be designed for intensive use during the week. This requires large storage rooms for the furnishings and equipment used in youth ministry as well as those used by other ministries meeting in this space. An outside entrance to the area, a serving kitchen, and toilet facilities are all important for weekday utilization.

Successful use of a gymnasium as the primary meeting space for teens is difficult to achieve. It may be possible by using gym-type carpet, acoustical treatment, a movable sound system, a dual lighting system, and enough storage to make a gym work. Most churches will have more practical, cost-effective alternatives.

Adults

Facility requirements for adult classes vary from church to church. One congregation had only two adult classes of several hundred each, both taught lecture style. Another church kept classes in a range of thirty to sixty so each would function as a "congregation" within the larger church. The most common pattern is to have a variety of class sizes and styles of teaching.

The trend in many larger, growing churches is to make home-based small groups the heart of their adult discipleship strategy. Some churches make adult Sunday school just one of several adult discipleship options available, with most groups meeting at other times. Some churches offer adult classes primarily for senior adults who are most comfortable with a traditional approach and encourage others to join groups that meet off campus or at the church during the week. Other churches offer occasional specialized classes on Sunday, such as new-member classes, and conduct all their adult discipleship groups at other times.

The shift from classroom-based to small group–based discipleship is primarily driven by ministry values: generally, small groups lead to deeper relationships and greater life change than classroom-based education. (Of course, some "Sunday school classes" are actually not classes as much as they are small groups who share life deeply and happen to meet on Sunday morning.) While your adult discipleship model should be driven primarily by your ministry vision and values, moving most adult discipleship from the classroom to the living room greatly decreases the need for classrooms.

Space allowances

The following space allowances are commonly used and can guide you in determining your space needs for education. Teachers and workers are counted along with their students. Space allowances are based on average attendance and allow room for 20 percent growth and occasional higher attendance. Area is based on wall-to-wall measurements.

Age Group	Space Needed per Person
Nursery, preschool,	30 sq. ft. each
and kindergarten	35 sq. ft. with large equipment
	25 sq. ft. minimum
Children	
Lower grades	25 sq. ft. each
	20 sq. ft. minimum
Upper grades	20 sq. ft. each
	15 sq. ft. minimum
Teens	
Class only	15 sq. ft. each (with tables)
Total multiuse	20 sq. ft. each
Adults	
At tables	15 sq. ft. each
Lecture class	12 sq. ft. each
	10 sq. ft. minimum

The rule of thumb is a total building area of fifty square feet per person, based on average attendance and single use of the facility. This does not include a gymnasium.

Study the space utilization of your present classes, based on average attendance, and adjust the above allowances to your specific methods and needs. The space needed per person is determined primarily by the method of teaching, the type of furniture, and how the furniture is being used.

Identify space wasters—large tables with seating on just one side, a large room with seating only around the walls, or overstuffed divans and chairs.

Buy lightweight six-foot tables (maximum size) so one person can fold and stack them. This is the best size for children's classes, seating six per table plus the teacher and a guest if needed. This size also gangs together best. For rooms that may at times be used by both children and adults, buy adjustable height tables so they can be changed quickly from children's use to adults' and back again.

Administration

For planning purposes, use a ratio of one equipping staff member (pastors and ministry directors) per 150 in average worship attendance unless you have developed your own ratio. Keep in mind that staff is added ahead of the next growth phase. A ratio of one office support staff member for every two equipping staff members is minimal if the equippers are to spend their time doing what they are educated and called to do rather than doing work that support staff can do faster, better, and more economically. The facility master plan must provide for expansion of administrative space as growth requires, either by converting adjacent space to offices or by adding on to the building. This is usually the first area to expand when growth takes place.

One facility need often overlooked is space for unpaid ministry leaders. The church that takes the ministry of the unpaid ministry leaders and office volunteers seriously enough to provide office space and equipment for them is more likely to be a growing church.

For specifics of office layout, see chapter 20, "Three Things Great Church Offices Do."

Recreation

In the forties and fifties, many churches said, "We want to minister to the youth of our church and community, so design us a *youth center*." In the sixties and seventies the big push was to build a *recreation center*. In the eighties and nineties the *family life center* was where the action was. I wonder what label we will invent next to describe what we build, because for all of the above we have built *gymnasiums*.

This was done with the best of intentions, but most of these churches built buildings to house nonexistent ministries. They assumed that if they built the buildings, people would use them. Most of the time these buildings were underutilized.

Build a gymnasium only if the church already has a strong recreation ministry and other facilities are not available. Before deciding on a gymnasium, do a careful cost-effectiveness study. To be cost-effective, a gym must be a multiuse facility, and that requires a first-class, expensive building. A bare-bones gym is a poor investment, because it will have very limited use.

It is rare for a church recreational program to be an effective outreach ministry. The potential is there, but remember: create the ministry first, then build the facility.

Parking

When street parking is not available, parking capacity limits growth more often than any other single facility restraint. A ratio of one car for every 2.5 people works in most areas. To find the car-to-people ratio in your church, count all the people in the building (including children, of course) and all the cars parked at the church. Assume that the ratio will go down and provide proportionally more parking spaces in the future. A ratio of one car for every two people, or even less, applies in some communities.

Without landscaping, you can park about 120 cars per acre; with landscaping, about one hundred per acre. Compact spaces can increase the ratio. Most cities and counties have specific parking lot requirements, such as landscaping and control of water runoff. Consult your planning and zoning department about requirements.

When you cannot add parking spaces, consider renting parking from nearby businesses that are closed during worship times, using remote parking with shuttle service, implementing stacked parking, and using your parking lot multiple times by having multiple services. Remember that worship and classes can be held at the same time only if there is enough parking available for both.

External Appearance

The outward appearance of your facilities should say, "We're open for business, and you're always welcome." The scale of the building should make people feel comfortable. A monumental, cathedral scale tends to do just the opposite.

The first way a facility can help welcome people is to invite them in through what they see. Landscaped parking, signs clearly identifying the entrances, driveways for drop-off and pick-up, and designated parking spaces for both Sunday and weekday visitors and handicap parking all tell visitors you have been looking forward to their arrival. Canopies marking both the Sunday and office entrances put the building in scale with people and provide shelter. The design uses sizes that make people feel comfortable, not over-powered, dominated, or awed. It avoids strong vertical elements, such as steeples, towers, and campaniles, in favor of horizontal lines and openings.

Your campus can be designed so that it is obvious to people passing by when your building is being used. People will gather on outdoor terraces where passersby can see them, not in hidden courtyards. Glass doors and walls at the entryways allow people outside to see people inside. Parking is visible from the street, not hidden behind the building, so it is obvious when the church is buzzing with activity.

At one church in the San Francisco area, the site plan included a soccer field, a picnic grove, a playground, and a gym placed at the front of the site where traditionally the sanctuary would be located. A parcourse, or exercise trail, is planned for the perimeter of the site. This is all for use by the community.

When the church campus looks inviting and open to the community, congregations are announcing to their neighbors, before they say a word, "We're open for business. You're always welcome here. Membership is not required."

Appendix B

More-with-Less Budgeting
for Building

The church had paid $24,000 for architect's drawings, and the drawings were gorgeous! Everyone in the room knew, though, that the spectacular building pictured on the church conference room wall would never be built. It cost far more than the church could afford. They were asking us to help them come up with a more cost-effective design. They were starting over from square one. Their $24,000 had been wasted, along with an enormous amount of time, energy, and momentum.

Obviously, it is foolish to pay an architect to create plans that cost more than your people can pay. A church should never wait for a contractor to bid on final construction plans to learn what it will cost. To avoid this costly mistake, prepare your building budget first, and then use it as a guide to decide on the scope of your project before starting the design and plans for your building.

Here is how one church did this.

Fruitvale Community Church was growing steadily and their existing buildings and site would soon reach maximum capacity. They decided to relocate and construct a new church campus.

Their goal was to build enough capacity that everyone could worship in a single service and then add more services as the church grew. In preparing their cost estimates, building committee members visited other churches in the community with newer buildings and similar occupancy. They asked about their planning and selection of an architect. They asked, "What would you do differently next time?" and "How did your architect control costs to stay within your budget?"

They also interviewed architects in their offices, inquiring about current costs of church construction and how the architects control cost to meet the budget. These are the numbers they came up with:

Requirements and Estimate of Costs

Occupancy: *1000*. (Ministry center seating 750 plus 250 children and youth.)

Size: *55,000 square feet*. (1,000 occupants at 50 square feet each = 50,000 square feet, the minimum building area for single-use architecture, plus a 5,000 square foot gymnasium.)

Building cost: *$5.5 million*. (55,000 square feet at $100/square foot. Adjust to current average cost of similar projects in your area.)

Parking: *400 cars*. (They counted cars during peak attendance and found the ratio of people to cars was 2.5 people per car. This number can vary from 1.7 to 3.0 depending on the church.)

Site size: *8 to 10 acres*. Acreage needed for buildings, parking, driveways, setbacks, storm water retention, and playground was 5 acres. They decided to buy 8 to 10 acres to provide room for growth. The real estate agent's cost estimate for the site was $1 million.

Project Cost Estimate

Site purchase	$1,000,000
Construction of buildings	$5,500,000
Additional costs	$1,903,000*
Total project cost	$8,403,000

*Estimate of additional project costs: construction contingency (3%) $165,000; permits, assessments, jurisdictional fees (1%) $55,000; fees for architect, engineers, consultants (acoustical, audiovisual, lighting), estimator, attorney (8%) $440,000; site development for utilities, storm water control, parking, walks, landscaping, playground, lighting, fencing, signs, etc. (10%) $550,000; furnishings, carpet, audiovisual equipment, window coverings, etc. (5%) $225,000; inflation for three years to start of construction (6%) $330,000; move-in, start-up, first-year increase of utilities/maintenance (1%) $55,000; project contingency (1%) $83,000.

A survey of the members and a study of the church's finances revealed that the potential for the additional giving to finance this amount did not exist. It was concluded that the financing would "steal" from funds for growth of ministries, staff, and outreach. In light of this, the members voted to develop a different design to reduce costs.

A New Design

The design adopted envisioned up to five services at different times and on different days to accommodate those who could not attend on Sunday and for outreach. An outreach service called The Table would use a café format with groups of six to eight eating together, visiting, sharing concerns, praying, and discussing the teaching presented by a leader. New people would be seated at tables with hosts who would welcome them and follow up with them during the week.

Multiple sessions of Christian education would greatly reduce the need for children's ministry space for Sunday morning. Some adult education would take place on Sunday morning, other groups would meet at the church during the week, and others would meet in homes.

Their multiuse ministry center would seat four hundred in worship and three hundred at tables for lectures or meals, and could be used as an open activity room. It would also have moveable sound-reducing walls to subdivide it into smaller spaces for a variety of uses including classrooms for their preschool.

Reduced Size and Cost

The new plan reduced the size of the building by about 40 percent in all areas except the offices. The master building plan provided for adding an activity room or gymnasium and other needs in the future. With these changes, the project cost estimate was reduced by at least 40 percent. With the sale of the existing campus, the cost would be reasonable for the church's giving level. Much of the cost would be covered by pledged giving to a provision fund before and during construction. Debt, if any, would be short-term and covered by renewing pledges. The ministry budget for the work of this growing church would not be limited by debt payments, changes in the economy, or unexpected events.

Notes

Chapter 1 The Possible Dream

1. Originally called Ray Bowman Consulting.

Chapter 2 To Accomplish More, Do (and Spend) Less

1. There are exceptions to this principle—paid staff, for example, and those whose schedules allow them to volunteer full-time.

Chapter 3 To Reach More People, Disband Your Evangelism Committee

1. Charles Arn, *How to Start a New Service* (Grand Rapids: Baker, 1997), Kindle edition.
2. For suggestions on making the most of your connections time, see chapter 18.
3. Christian Schwarz, *Natural Church Development* (St. Charles, IL: ChurchSmart Resources, 1996). The Natural Church Development survey is an excellent tool for measuring your church's health, identifying areas of needed growth, and tracking progress as you address growth areas. Partnering with a trained Natural Church Development coach during this process increases the church's improvement in health by an average of 50 percent.

Chapter 4 To Make More Disciples, "Teach" Less

1. Robert E. Coleman, *The Master Plan of Evangelism*, rev. ed. (Grand Rapids: Revell, 1993), 24–25.
2. Adapted from Lawrence O. Richards, *Christian Education* (Grand Rapids: Zondervan, 1975), 84–85.
3. Richards, *Christian Education*, 45. Italics in original.

4. Ibid., 113–14. Italics in original.

5. Greg Ogden, *Transforming Discipleship: Making Disciples a Few at a Time* (Downers Grove, IL: InterVarsity, 2003), 9.

6. Ibid.

7. Ibid., 146.

8. Ibid., 43.

9. A similar approach to discipleship triads is Neil Cole's Life Transformation Groups, which include a heavy focus on reading Scripture as well as a strategy of multiplication.

Chapter 5 To Empower for Ministry, Ax Committees

1. This introduction to the five kinds of teams just scratches the surface. For more on the five types of teams, see www.morewithlesschurch.com.

2. An excellent guide for beginning to refocus your board from management to governance is *High-Impact Church Boards* by T. J. Addington (NavPress, 2010). A more in-depth technical resource is *Winning on Purpose* by John Edmund Kaiser (Abingdon, 2006).

Chapter 6 To Multiply Leadership, Recruit Fewer Leaders

1. The term "working group" comes from *The Wisdom of Teams* by Jon R. Katzenbach and Douglas K. Smith (New York: Harper Business, 1999). They also refer to a working group as a "single-leader group."

2. For more on nurturing team culture, see www.morewithlesschurch.com.

3. The Hartford Center for Religion Research summarizes their research findings: "According to the survey, congregations with leaders who have seminary education are, as a group, far more likely to report that in their congregations they perceive less clarity of purpose; more and different kinds of conflict; less person-to-person communication; less confidence in the future and more threat from changes in worship." (Carl S. Dudley and David A. Roozen, *Faith Communities Today: A Report on Religion in the Unites States Today*, Hartford Institute for Religion Research, Hartford Seminary, March 2001, 67.) Research by the Institute for Natural Church Development found that "formal theological training has a negative correlation to both church growth and overall quality of churches." (Christian A. Schwarz, *Natural Church Development* [St. Charles, IL: ChurchSmart Resources, 1996], 25.)

4. See "Four Marks of a Disciple-Making Relationship," page 37.

Chapter 7 To Improve Health, Stir Up Conflict

1. Pat Kiefert, "The NetResults Research: Church Fights and Outreach," *Net Results* (January 1996), 26.

Chapter 8 To Increase Unity, Throw Out Your Vision Statement

1. Aubrey Malphurs, *Values-Driven Leadership: Discovering and Developing Your Core Values for Ministry* (Grand Rapids: Baker, 1996), 32.

2. Patrick Lencioni, *The Advantage* (San Francisco: Jossey-Bass, 2012), 93–98.

3. Riverside Church is part of The Christian and Missionary Alliance.

4. Lencioni, *The Advantage*, 99–104. Lencioni describes here a process for isolating core values from other values.

Chapter 10 Hire Equippers to Multiply Leaders

1. For sample job descriptions of these positions and suggestions for interviewing for these positions, see www.morewithlesschurch.com.

Chapter 11 The Case of the Overpaid Secretary

1. The spiritual gift survey we use is *Discover Your God-Given Gifts* by Don and Katie Fortune (rev. ed. Revell, 2009), also available through our website, www.living-stones.com.

Chapter 12 Build a Dream Team

1. Patrick Lencioni, *The Five Dysfunctions of a Team* (San Francisco: Jossey-Bass, 2002).

2. John Edmund Kaiser, *Winning on Purpose* (Nashville: Abingdon, 2006), 83. Kaiser calls this approach Accountable Leadership. He acknowledges that there are a number of other respected governance models.

3. For a description of the responsibilities of a governing board see *High-Impact Church Boards* by T. J. Addington or *Winning on Purpose* by John Edmund Kaiser.

Chapter 13 Confessions of a Surprised Architect

1. Richard Foster, *The Freedom of Simplicity* (San Francisco: Harper & Row, 1981), 153–54.

Chapter 18 Adding a New Service

1. The next chapter explains how to structure double-session Sunday school with little need for more workers.

2. Other options include multisite, multivenue, church planting, and adding a fourth service.

Chapter 21 One Church, Multiple Locations

1. Warren Bird, "Big News—Multisite Churches Now Number More Than 5000" Leadership Network, August 22, 2012, leadnet.org//blog/post/big_news_multisite _churches_now_number_more_than_5000.

2. www.northcoastchurch.com.

Chapter 22 When It's Time to Build

1. More on how to form the church health team, length of service, and team responsibilities can be found at www.morewithlesschurch.com.

Chapter 26 From Vision to Provision

1. Giving Rocket is a coaching program to help churches increase weekly giving. For more information visit therocketcompany.com.

2. Financial data is derived from eighty-five churches that consulted with Living Stones Associates from 1998–2012.

Contributors

Mike Hare (ch. 7) spent more than twenty-five years pastoring four turnaround churches before planting a church. Spending decades cleaning up the wreckage of churches that had mishandled conflict prompted him to earn a PhD in conflict analysis and resolution to help churches navigate conflict in life-giving ways. Since 2003, Mike has headed LSA's Church Conflict Consulting Track. Mike is also Staff Chaplain at Compassion International. He and his wife, Colleen, live in Colorado Springs.

Dennis Hesselbarth (ch. 10) recently completed twenty-six years as the founding pastor of Hilltop Urban Church in Wichita, Kansas. He has been a part of the LSA team as a specialist in cross-cultural ministry since 2009. He and his wife, Joy, live in Bremerton, Washington.

Peggy Heid (ch. 26) and her husband, Brent, have planted two churches while also heading up their family business. Peggy has been a part of the LSA team since 2008, serving as a generalist (ministries, staffing, facilities, and finances) with particular passion and expertise in the area of finances and stewardship. She is on staff at her home church, Vox Dei Community in Raymore, Missouri, as the connections ministry director.

About the Authors

The relationship among this book's three authors is unique. **Ray Bowman** founded the ministry that is now called Living Stones Associates (LSA) in 1980. When Ray retired in 2000, **Eddy Hall** succeeded him and now leads a team of ten consultants. **Skipp Machmer** is being groomed to succeed Eddy as team leader. Ray is in his eighties, Eddy is in his early sixties, and Skipp is in his thirties. This book is coauthored by LSA's three generations of leadership with contributions by other team members.

Living Stones Associates (and its predecessor Ray Bowman Consulting) has conducted consultations with hundreds of churches in more than thirty denominations throughout the United States and Canada. In addition to the Integrated Planning Track (ministries, staffing, facilities, and finances), the team offers a Church Health Consulting track and a Church Conflict Consulting track, plus specialized leadership training and coaching in various aspects of congregational life.

Ray Bowman left his architectural practice after thirty years to follow God's call to consult with churches. After decades of encouraging churches to build, Ray began using his experience to help churches avoid unnecessary building through more creative use of their existing facilities. Sally, Ray's wife, joined him as a partner in the consulting. They learned that this kind of facility planning could not be done in a vacuum but had to be the result of a comprehensive assessment. Effective planning must integrate all four dimensions of the church's life: ministries, staffing, facilities, and finances.

With Eddy Hall, Ray coauthored two books including *When Not to Build: An Architect's Unconventional Wisdom for the Growing Church* (Baker, 1992, 2000), and their articles have appeared in more than fifty church-related periodicals.

Ray's pioneering work in the '80s and '90s led to the formation of the Living Stones Associates consulting team. Now retired, Ray and Sally live in Olathe, Kansas.

Eddy Hall began working with Ray as a writer in 1986. In 1996 he joined the consulting team and assumed leadership of LSA in 2000. Since then the team has grown to include ten consultants from many denominations and with a wide range of professional specialties.

Eddy also leads the staff team of Hilltop Urban Church, a multiethnic congregation in a low-income neighborhood in Wichita, Kansas, where he serves in the areas of his greatest passion: indigenous leadership development, team building, and navigating change. He and his wife, Laura, live in Wichita.

Skipp Machmer is the executive pastor of programming and strategic development at Riverside Church in Big Lake, Minnesota. Prior to becoming executive pastor he served as creative arts pastor. He first connected with Living Stones in 2005, when Riverside asked LSA to partner with them in developing an integrated plan to remove barriers to growth. In 2008, after Riverside implemented that plan, Living Stones worked with Riverside to develop a second integrated plan.

Skipp brings a wide range of experience to LSA including expertise in building teams, both paid and volunteer, and in planning, producing, and leading worship services and evangelistically fruitful community outreach efforts. He is experienced in leading churches through directional changes related to worship and technology, in helping churches transition from being inwardly focused to outwardly focused, and navigating conflict. Skipp and his wife, Cherise, live in the Twin Cities area with their three daughters, Abby, Elle, and Izzy.

Every Church Faces
DEFINING MOMENTS

- *Building Decisions*
- *Plateau or Decline*
- *Divisive Conflict*
- *Lack of Shared Vision*

Your response to these critical times will shape **your church's future.**

At an UNFAMILIAR CROSSROAD, nothing takes the place of an EXPERIENCED GUIDE.

Since 1980, Living Stones consultants have partnered with hundreds of congregations in more than thirty denominations throughout the United States. and Canada. Living Stones has a long track record of helping churches increase ministry effectiveness through strategic planning and coaching in four critical areas—ministries, staffing, facililties, and finances.

As you weigh the crucial decisions that will shape your church's future, could you use an experienced guide?

LIVING STONES associates

helping churches navigate change

www.living-stones.com